WHAT OTHERS ARE SAYING

The author presents teachable moments that highlight the level of ethical responsibility and care leaders must take to make well-informed decisions that positively impact others. His focus on individual people doing the right thing extends to a culture of organizational excellence! This is truly an instructional text for developing the *leadership gene* in individuals, and these lessons can be applied across industries. (Janelle Elias, MAEd, higher education administrator, accreditation director at University of Phoenix)

What a superbly distinguishing contribution this volume is to the literature on leadership! The book *The Leadership Gene* by John DiCicco is a modern-day classic of extraordinary quality and validity. The content and style of the book is on the cutting edge of leadership development, both in theory and practice.

I enthusiastically recommend this book *The Leadersip Gene* for in service and preservice leadership training programs. Leaders in corporate and public service organizations, as well as universities would find this book to be a most valuable and significant tool at all levels of the leadership training spectrum. It is a powerful book indeed!

—Robert L. Heichberger, PhD, award-winning author, distinguished professor-director emeritus of leadership, SUNY Fredonia and Capella University

The ilk of a true leader denotes that he/she is strong, determined and humble; always willing to learn from all sources. As well, a leader at times must have the ability to show empathy, sympathy, care and respect.

That being said, I appreciate professor DiCicco's visionary work as it provides knowledge and brilliant insight on developing the leader within you.

—William G. Gross
Boston Police Superintendent-in-Chief

Some say leadership cannot be learned. John DiCicco's approach in this wonderful new book suggests we can all be better people first and ultimately achieve leadership success. He presents a winning formula for people in all walks of life.

—Jordan Rich Chart
Productions, Inc. WBZ Radio

I enjoy the story telling style the author uses to help us all find our own Leadership Gene. It makes it easy for me to understand the message which is we all have leadership capability. It may be seen by others around us first, but in order for us to find our own, we must be willing to make changes, accept and understand them. This book will help you do that. Happy reading.

—Patricia M. Comeau
Human Resources
Reebok International Ltd.

In my profession it is important to be disciplined, dedicated to your craft and most of all goal oriented. At the end of each chapter John presents us with leadership lessons designed to help us continuously develop ways to improve our leadership skills. His book over and over again emphasizes the fact that leaders never stop learning and there is always room to grow.

—Peter Rappoli, MS, CCS, CSCS
Owner Elite Health and Fitness Center

THE
LEADERSHIP
GENE

JOHN DICICCO

THE
LEADERSHIP
GENE

UNION SQUARE
PUBLISHING

Published by
Union Square Publishing
301 E. 57th Street, 4th floor
New York, NY 10022
www.unionsquarepublishing.com

Copyright © 2017 by John A. DiCicco

All rights reserved. No part of this book may be reproduced or transmitted in any form or by in any means, electronic or mechanical, including photocopying, recording, or by any information storage and retrieval system, without the written permission of the Publisher, except where permitted by law.

Manufactured in the United States of America, or in the United Kingdom when distributed elsewhere.

DiCicco, John
    The Leadership Gene
    LCCN: 2017952774
    ISBN: 978-1-946928-13-9
    eBook: 978-1-946928-15-3

Cover design by: Joe Potter
Interior design: Jomar Ouano
Photo credits: Gerry Evelyn / Evelyn Images

www.johndicicco.com

DEDICATION

I would like to dedicate this book to a dear friend and colleague, Mr. William Dausey. He gave me the inspiration to write this story and the encouragement to include his many years of experience in the lesson plans contained within. I will be forever grateful to his contributions as a scholar, leader, and humanitarian.

CONTENTS

Foreword 13
Chapter 1: Setting the Stage 15
Chapter 2: Meeting by Accident 23
Chapter 3: The Awakening 39
Chapter 4: The Morning After the Day Before 53
Chapter 5: Time to Face the Music 61
Chapter 6: Lost in Translation 71
Chapter 7: Finding the Answers 79
Chapter 8: Finding the Leadership Gene 91
Chapter 9: The Dichotomy of Perception 105
Chapter 10: Managers Delegate the Facts and Leaders Question Them When Appropriate 115
Chapter 11: Bringing the Leadership Gene Out of Dormancy 125
Chapter 12: The Human Connection Gene Makes Its Mark 139
Chapter 13: My Leadership Gene and I Are One 151
References 159

FOREWORD

Within every human being, there is a powerful force that lies dormant until it is brought out by something or someone. I call this force the leadership gene. This gene does not need any type of validation to exist. The reader can decide whether or not leaders are born or leaders are made. In either case, every human being has a primal instinct to survive and flourish from the moment they are born until the moment they choose to do something with that instinct or not.

In my first book, *Leadership Is a Choice*, my coauthor and I decided to assume that leaders make choices to lead. This book is about something inside of all of us that can be developed if the right elements exist externally or internally to manifest his or her leadership gene. This gene can influence the behavior of others either negatively or positively. This book explains about making choices for the right reasons and perhaps not for the right reasons. These choices are up to us.

The author believes that everyone has a dominant leadership gene nested among many other leadership traits. The talents and skills of an effective mentor can help bring out and develop that gene if the owner of the gene chooses to uncover its potential. Finally, the gene owner and the mentor collaboratively decide to utilize that gene for their purposes and the development of others who choose to bring their genes out of dormancy. In essence, the mentee who develops his or her leadership gene becomes the mentor to someone else to develop their dominant gene if they so choose.

This book is about successorship, mentorship, and life in general. Yes, leadership is not just about business; it's about life. We choose to lead our lives by what we perceive to be true. We choose to influence our own lives and the lives of others by choices that we make. The leadership gene helps us make those choices and helps us decide who we are and what we are doing in our journey through life. Can you find your leadership gene? Read on and discover the force within you that perhaps you never thought was lying dormant for so long. Take this journey with Josh Keating and find the Josh Keating in you. Can you relate to his character? Or are you Lynn Ann Marconi? Perhaps you are Jonathan or Russell? Keep reading and learn about the characters I've just named.

I wish each and every one of you continued success in your path through life and how you lead yourself and others. You are successful, and you will find your leadership gene.

—John

Chapter 1

SETTING THE STAGE

The flight from Boston was long, and I had not had anything to eat since I got on the plane six and a half hours ago. I am tired and hungry but determined to get to my appointment a half hour early to settle into my surroundings. I could relax prior to the most important job interview of my life. Despite my fatigue, I am focused and ready to face the potential challenges that accompany every interview vying for the position of chief financial officer.

Medical Solutions Incorporated is a Fortune 500 company located only 2.5 miles from LAX where I just landed. I have heard nothing but good things about this company and have researched it thoroughly before I decided to see what it really has to offer me. What I discovered in my research was that Medical Solutions started out as a private office in 1972 for local doctors who wanted to experiment with new and innovative medicines that would provide affordable treatments for those that could not afford the more expensive brand-name drugs. Of course, all of the drugs that they created would be approved by the FDA prior to distribution.

    The concept really took off and within three years' time, Innovative Drug Research Inc. was a public offering. With more than 450 employees, stocks were selling at $20.64 per share. This was in 1977. Here it is in 2013, and Innovative Drug Research Inc. is now Medical Solutions with over 2,400 employees worldwide and the stock is at $52.34 per share. This is a certain possibility for me to move up in my field, if I am lucky enough to get the opportunity.

    I will be meeting Mr. Jonathan Peters, the company's CEO at 11 a.m. for the second round of interviews which will be held between 10:00 a.m. and 6:00 p.m. today. The first round of interviews were for screening and were very long telephone interviews lasting over ninety minutes each. I had three of them, starting with a human resources representative and moving up to a vice president, which got me to where I am right now. However, for now, let's focus on me getting off the plane at LAX. It is Friday, March 15, 2013 at 9:35 a.m., Los Angeles time, and I have plenty of time to get to my appointment.

    After bringing down my traveling bag and laptop from the overhead of the plane, I quickly found myself thanking the airline staff for a smooth ride and am now going down the connecting ramp to the airport terminal checking my e-mails on my blackberry to see if I missed anything important while I was on the plane. My BlackBerry buzzes with over eighteen messages. I figured I could use a quick cup of coffee and then continue reading all of my messages. I could answer all of these calls that need my immediate attention. I can do this before my meeting with Peters.

I spot a Starbucks coffee station just outside the landing terminal and begin walking toward Starbucks as I am checking my BlackBerry for more messages when I inadvertently collide with a "Wait Here" sign and immediately look up thus breaking my concentration. Upon looking up and away heading for the Starbucks coffee station, I had my eyes locked in utter astonishment at what they were observing. Without a doubt, I am looking at what appears to be a replica of the back of the head of my boss, Lynn Anne Marconi, our new director of operations at Biotech Medical in Boston, my present employer. I did not know she had a trip planned to the West Coast this week. I cannot avoid crossing her path to anywhere I needed to go in the airport at the present time. So I have two choices: Wait at the airport until she boards her aircraft back to Boston, which is about one hour from now and be late for my meeting with Mr. Peters. Or I could approach her with a friendly greeting and make up some type of excuse of why I am here at LAX during the work week. I have to make this decision soon. I am not one to enjoy confrontation. However, I have to do something since I have this meeting at 11:00 a.m. today!

Time is of the essence as I check my watch and realize it is now 10:05 a.m. This gives me only thirty minutes to get to my destination, get settled, and be ready for my interview at 11:00 a.m. with Mr. Peters. I nervously begin to calculate a strategy, which I would have to make very soon. I decide to go to my destination and try to avoid making eye contact with my boss. This is a big mistake on my part! As I was trying to walk feverishly past Lynn Anne, she decided to observe the flight changes that were located on a large display at the back of my head as I was walking toward her. Lynn and I immediately made eye contact, truly surprised to see each other. Lynn says to me, "Josh Keating, what are you doing here?" I need to make something up real quick, and I don't know what to say. In a split second, it goes through my head that I need to get myself out of this terminal and ready for my interview. What else could have happened to me this morning? Is this a conspiracy to keep me from going on this interview? Is my perseverance being tested? I am now a lot less focused than I was ten minutes ago. I am very nervous now and feel unprepared for my meeting. I needed to get out of this terminal, and I needed to do it quickly. What am I going to do? For the second I am casting my eyes on Lynn Anne and my whole world is turning upside down.

At that moment, I felt persecuted and wanted to stick my head in the sand at the same time. I had no choice but to walk by Lynn Anne and head for the terminal exit. There were no other options as I reminded myself to be cool. I am usually not a patient person by nature, and I admit I have an impulsive flair. Here goes my best efforts to get by Lynne Ann. This is just so embarrassing, yet I tried to remain focused. As I kept my eyes focused on the terminal door exit, and just ready to exit the terminal door to hail a cab for an appointment less than three miles away, I hear Lynne calling to me and saying, "Josh, wait up!" I try to ignore that I hear her and keep walking abruptly toward the door. She was starting to run toward me and said, "Josh, we need to talk. I need you to cover this meeting for me." She is now three feet behind me, and I couldn't avoid the fact that I hear her talking to me unless I suddenly went deaf!

I cannot escape Lynn and I nervously and abruptly turn around with a very distant, forced smile on my face as I am perspiring as if I ran the marathon. I could feel my newly and freshly starched shirt from early this morning getting more saturated with perspiration from this encounter on top of the six-hour plane flight. I am a mess, and it is now, 10:22 a.m., and I am still at the airport. Lynne, after catching up with me, stated, "Josh, I just got a call from Boston. I have to get back to meet a client at 8:00 p.m. this evening for dinner and I can't miss my flight. Boston wants me to cover this meeting here this afternoon at 2:30 Pacific time, which will be 5:30 p.m. Eastern Standard Time. I was ready to tell them that I would have to cancel, and I see you. This is like a Godsend." I look at Lynn with amazement, disillusionment, and astonishment all at the same time. I am a basket case and a loser all at the same time. It is now 10:25. Lynn suggests that we go and sit at a table nearby to discuss her meeting at 2:30.

I feel as if as if am a dead duck. I need to somehow reschedule my appointment with Jonathan Peters. Lynn goes into all of the detail of the meeting but never mentions or asks me why I am here in LA. I don't volunteer the information either. This is really a bizarre situation! Lynn, after explaining all of the details of her alleged 2:30 p.m. meeting, was now being called to her flight for boarding. She gave me a hug and told me that she will never forget that I am doing her this favor. She stated she will catch up with me later. Now, off she goes for boarding.

I immediately dialed Jonathan whom I am told is at a meeting and will not be through with this meeting until 12:30 p.m. This will never give me enough time to reschedule my appointment with him. I needed time to think now on what to do. If I had been a little more prudent with my time, I may not have been in the storm I am in right now! At any rate, I redialed my appointment and asked for Mr. Peter's personal secretary. She picked up the phone and told me that Mr. Peters had already scheduled all the interviews he'll hold personally to fill this position. There will not be another opportunity to reschedule for an interview unless there was nobody in this group that he will interview for a second time. Basically, she's telling me that today is all I got to see Peters personally. So she told me to figure out how to get to the office today, for my scheduled appointment.

Okay, you're probably wondering why I am on an interview and not really happy or proud of what I am doing by going on this interview. As my story unfolds, you will get your answers. However, for the present time, let me tell you a little bit about my present employer, Medical Solutions Inc.

Medical Solutions Inc. started its business in 1975. Not long after Biotech Medical Inc. began its business in 1972. Medical Solutions did not grow as rapidly as Biotech Medical. However, the company began as a medical transcription company that was privately owned and also grew to a publicly traded organization. By 1980, Medical Solutions retained its identity before it went public, however expanded its business to include drug research for manufacturing generic drugs at a fraction of the cost charged by major drug manufacturers of the most common drugs approved by the FDA. I work on the accounting end of the business and report to the director of operations. My present boss, Lynn Ann Marconi, is the new director of operations, replacing Mike Feeney, who is out indefinitely on medical leave.

LEADERSHIP LESSONS

We've only observed a few minutes of Josh's life, but can we discern any clues to his leadership abilities? Would you go to work for Josh, expecting him to lead you to success and help you develop your talents?

- A leader needs to plan have a firm grasp of priorities, keeping his eyes on the goal at all times. Given that, would you have taken the early morning flight to LA, or would you have flown out the night before? Josh's goal is a CFO position and the interview with Mr. Peters is the most direct route to his objective. Instead of focusing on the goal, Josh decided to spend the night at home in Boston. At best, he will arrive for his interview exhausted from his early departure and rumpled from a transcontinental flight.

- A leader understands that plans rarely proceed smoothly and is always ready with a contingency plan when things go awry. This allows him to adjust plans on the flight to keep on track to his goal. Running into one's boss in the airport is something we may not expect, but late arrivals are not a rare occurrence. Josh left himself less than ninety minutes to get from the airport to his appointment. Much of that time would be needed to disembark, walk through the concourse and terminal, stand in the taxi line, and go 2.5 miles through LA traffic. If the plane were only a few minutes late, he would miss his appointment.

- A leader must be consistently honorable and trustworthy. Running into one's boss in the airport on the way to a job interview is certainly a difficult situation, but trying to duck the confrontation is not an action that inspires confidence and honesty.

Watch Josh's thoughts and actions in the coming chapters, and gain a deeper understanding of the nature of leadership.

Chapter 2

MEETING BY ACCIDENT

There is no way I am going to make my meeting with Jonathan considering the time restraints that were put on me by Lynn to cover her meeting. I now feel like a dishrag totally discombobulated and confused and, facing one of the biggest dilemmas of my life. I do know that if I don't come through for Lynn, I will have to disclose to her what I was doing in LA. I also know that if I miss this meeting, I probably would have missed one of the biggest opportunities for my career in my lifetime. Right now, I am tripping over my own feet, and I don't know what to do.

Okay, now let me think this through. *What is the big deal if I really miss this meeting with Jonathan? Is it the end of the world? I think not. I'll cover for Lynn at this meeting, and I'll be a hero in her eyes. This will make up for all the times that she thought I was a screw up and mediocre at my job. She will think different of me now, and perhaps I may even get a chance to get ahead in my company with her support. Who am I kidding? This will never happen. I know what she thinks of me and being in her good graces will only be a temporary thing until the next crisis comes along.*

Deep down, I can now convince myself that this is the best option for me to be safe, and now, I have a good job waiting for me back in Boston after I finish this meeting. There will always be other opportunities to interview for good jobs. I am still young but still have a lot to learn, and it's important for me to be able to pay my bills and live rather comfortably. Just let me sit here and wait for our clients to meet me as Lynn has already made the arrangements for me while she's en route to Boston to have dinner with another client. Okay, I'm sitting in a rather good place right next to the checkout area and reception area. I have a good identification of the client, and I will be ready to greet her when she arrives in a few minutes. I begin checking my e-mails once again and noticed that there is a flight to Boston with a connection in Kansas City that will be leaving at two o'clock this afternoon Pacific time.

At the time I read about the Boston flight, I get up to grab something to eat and make a quick visit to the restroom. I returned to my seat and didn't realize how much time had passed from the time I was worried about making my meeting with Jonathan for my scheduled interview and how close it was to the time I was supposed to meet Lynn's clients at 2:00 p.m. Yes, it was already 1:35 p.m. Pacific time, and my client would be arriving to greet Lynn (now me) in the next twenty minutes or so. Little did I know that Jonathan Peters had an emergency call that one of his family members was suddenly taken very ill, and he had to fly home and postpone his scheduled interviews. Little did I know that my interview, had I made it on time, would have been canceled anyway and would have to be rescheduled.

As far as I was concerned, I missed the interview, and therefore, there will be no other options for me to interview with Jonathan. I would have to wait for another potential job opportunity to come up before I would have to go through so much risk to take a day off to leave my job and come out of my comfort zone. Boy that was a relief.

It is almost 1:40 p.m., Pacific time, and I am now taking my last sip of coffee, and I think I will just close my eyes for a minute and reflect on my future discussion with Lynn's clients. Yes, I am a loyal employee of my present company and the way I feel right now. I plan to be that way for a long time. Well, as fate has it, this is not always the case! I look up in the distance. I see what appears to be the description that Lynn had given me on what one of her clients would be wearing and what she would look like. I am now thinking that I see her. I get up slowly, grab my briefcase, and begin walking slowly at the airline that Lynn told me her client would be flying in from where I see a crowd of passengers exiting the aircraft. It was flight 237 from Chicago to LAX that would be taking off on a direct route to Boston at 3:45 p.m., Pacific time, arriving in Boston at 12:17 a.m. Eastern Standard Time. Little did I know that Jonathan Peters would be on that flight to Boston's Brigham and Women's Hospital to see his sister.

As I walked toward the direction of the plane to meet Lynn's client, I passed by a ticketing station and was stopped so that passengers could exit flight 237 and await boarding for new passengers to fly from LAX directly to Boston. I usually don't pay attention to what is being said around me when I am focused on something else. For some reason, I heard a ticketing agents say to a passenger, "Can I help you?"

The voice on the other end said, "I don't have any luggage, and I need a ticket to Boston on this flight."

I heard the ticket agent asked, "May I have your name?"

The gentleman replied, "Jonathan Peters." I gasped when I heard the name. This had to be too much of a coincidence to be the same person that I was to interview with more that two hours ago. I was speechless and could not say anything.

I did not want to be impulsive and asked if he was the same person I was to interview with earlier today. I would look foolish out of place, and he would know that I would've missed my appointment. Additionally, I had no idea why he was at the airport when he should be at work interviewing people. I didn't know what to do, so I kept walking looking for Lynn's client who when I got close to the individual was not the person I had to meet. Although it looks like her from a distance, I still cannot find her, and I am just sitting in the area where passengers are continuing to come out of flight 237 until the last person just came out of the plane. I still am not seeing Lynn's client.

At any rate, I just waited and thought about what I needed to do next. At this point, my entire ego is turned inside out and upside down. My emotions are at a heightened level, and I feel like I want to jump out of my skin. Here I am sitting waiting for a client of my boss's that never shows up off the plane that I was to meet with fifteen minutes ago. It is now 2:15 p.m., Pacific time, and there is no client. I am not at work for any reason my boss is aware of, nor does she know why I am here in LA, and the man I was going to interview with for a job is sitting one hundred feet away from me in the same airport ready to board a plane. Yes, my ticket to a high-caliber and very well-paying job is sitting at the very airport a hundred feet from me boarding a plane back to Boston. Why? I have no idea!

I am now frozen in time and space and caught up all in myself and ready to scream as result of the giant panic attack. Suddenly, for no apparent reason, something comes over me and calms me down. It is like a second wind that I never felt before in my life. I am able to focus and pull myself together and realize that it is not the end of the world if this trip to LA does not work out. I am an intelligent, capable human being who would be able to use this experience as a learning curve and "take it to the next level. I realize that I didn't need anyone else to tell me to accept my inner self. I didn't have to apologize for what I felt, nor did I have to validate it to anyone. After thinking this, I got a phone call from Lynn telling me that her client missed her flight and would have to reschedule her appointment. Lynn thanked me and told me to have dinner on the company and take my time coming back. She even told me I could take the next day off if I had things to do. She also told me she would not forget that I had gone out on the limb and sacrificed my day to accommodate hers.

As I began walking out of the airport, with my eyes on the exit gate, I noticed that the gentleman who identified himself as Jonathan Peters was sitting down, waiting for his flight to board. I was so tempted to go over and talk to him and ask him if he worked for Medical Solutions where I was to interview for a job earlier that morning. I think not. I think I should just leave things alone and play it safe while I still can. Let's face it. I am still in Lynn's good graces. I have a job when I go back in. I really don't have to explain myself as to why I was in LA. She probably assumes it was some family matter. I can do this. I can leave well enough alone.

Well, as fate has it, as I am walking by Jonathan Peters, I noticed that he had dropped his itinerary on the ground and was attempting to pick it up. As he went to pick up his itinerary, he dropped his jacket out of his hand. Should I walk by him? Or should I look him in the eye, pick up his jacket, put it in his hand, and introduce myself? This is my choice. This is my one moment in time that could change my life forever.

One million thoughts are now running through my mind as the twenty seconds it took for me to walk by Jonathan seemed like an eternity, especially when I saw him drop his jacket on the ground. He seemed very flustered and frustrated, and it would not appear to be the best time to introduce yourself to someone. However, just three minutes ago, when I felt so stressed and out of sorts with myself where I actually wanted to jump out of my skin, this amazing silence and control came over me, which put everything in perspective. Well, it's happening to me again. I am thrusting forward without thinking to pick up Mr. Peters's coat and return it to his hand. In the process, we are bumping heads together and nearly knock each other out. We are both looking at each other in amazement and simultaneously laughing hysterically over the incident.

Well, this is how the story begins with Jonathan Peters. I purposely wrote the dialogue above in the present tense so you would capture my experiences with my future mentor which led my road to becoming what I believe is a successful leader and mentor to so many future leaders.

Jonathan quickly thanked me for picking up his jacket, and as he laughed, he also thanked me for giving him such a bump on the head. He also told me that he wasn't going to sue me for battery as it was in the line of duty. I heartedly laughed when he made this comment and introduced myself as Josh Keating, realizing I was supposed to interview with him this morning as I stated my name. Jonathan looked up at me quite puzzled with a very mysterious frown on his face and said, "No, you're not the Jonathan Keating I was supposed to be interviewing this morning, right?" He stated that that would be too much of a coincidence because if I was that person, he really owes me a big apology. I looked at Jonathan in a very puzzling way and almost had to restrain myself to say anything that would put my foot in my mouth.

I figured, *What the heck?* "Yes, Mr. Peters." Taking a deep breath, I stated, "I was supposed to meet with you at eleven o'clock." I took a deep breath, and I instinctively said, "I guess that didn't happen, obviously, because you are here at the airport boarding a flight to Boston."

Peter's shot a response right back to me and stated, "Funny, I walked by the reception area, about 11:00 a.m. and didn't see you waiting." He had a big grin on his face. He stated, "Most people applying for these types of positions usually are pretty nervous and try to get to the interview early." I told him that I probably headed for the bathroom. That's why he didn't see me. He smiled again with that wide grin on his face. "That's where I was heading!" I gave up at that point and didn't belabor the matter. It wasn't really doing me very much justice.

Jonathan next asked me if I was I heading any place in particular since my interview had to be rescheduled. I didn't know what to say at this point since I already spoke with his assistant and told her about my dilemma at the airport and that I might be late for the interview. Before I could answer, Jonathan advised me that his secretary would be getting with anyone that had an interview with him at 11:00 a.m. or after. Since he was notified about a close family member at 10:00 a.m. and didn't get to tell his secretary until 10:45 a.m., I thought it might be best at this point to leave well enough alone and change the subject.

I finally was able to book a flight to Boston at 8:30 p.m., Pacific time, arriving at 5:00 a.m. the following day, Eastern Standard Time. Jonathan's was booked on flight 764 to Boston at 5:00 p.m. Pacific time. If he let me, this would be my opportunity now to chat with Jonathan. *What would I say to him? How would I begin the conversation?* This would feel so awkward to me that the man I am supposed to interview with just hours ago is now sitting next to me, one on one, and I have his undivided attention, maybe. This will be my opportunity to really get to know him.

I don't even know if he wants to talk. I don't even know why he's going back to Boston. I know absolutely nothing about him. And here I am sitting next to the guy that could be my future boss. This is nuts! I reminded myself again that I have to calm down and put this all in perspective. I am only sitting here talking to another person who is in flight, just as I am, and flying to Boston for reasons that we both don't know, other than ourselves.

So how do I break the ice with Jonathan? Should I tell him why I was even here? Should I be discreet and just make conversation about sports and tell him about my family and friends? Here again, I don't even know why he is flying to Boston. *Maybe, I should start off with that in the conversation. Do I even go there?*

After I booked my flight, I returned to the waiting area where Jonathan was sitting and sat across from him. He was reading his flight itinerary and did not look up at me. I then cleared my throat, and he looked at me and signaled me to come and sit next to him. I got up slowly, picked up my briefcase, and went to sit next to him. There was a long silence for about five minutes as he was reading through some notes he had written on a small tablet of paper. I noticed that his handwriting was very neat, and he was very structured on what he was writing. However, he made no attempt to hide what he was writing from me. He seemed pretty open and relaxed. He asked me if I wanted anything to eat or drink and said he was going to the restroom and asked if I would watch his briefcase for him. I thought to myself, *How could this man trust a perfect stranger?* I thought this was quite bizarre as I could've run off with his briefcase at any time.

I told Jonathan. I didn't want anything to eat, and I would be happy to watch his briefcase. He smiled at me and walked toward the restroom with a brisk step. I was truly amazed that he trusted me perhaps with some very important documents in his briefcase. This says a lot about the man that just walked away from me. If this is the man that I was going to work for if my interviews were successful, I would be a very lucky man for so many different reasons.

When Jonathan returned, he asked me what my plans were with my present company and why I was interviewing with this company for a job. I told him that I needed to change my venue. I told him that I wanted a challenge beyond my present job responsibilities and sometimes changes are necessary in life to get ahead. Jonathan looked at me in a very puzzling manner and said, "Is that so?" Then he looked up at me and just stared intensely at me, scratched his head a bit, and then asked me, "Why do you think change is so important?" Then he stretched a bit and asked me, "What is so wrong in trying to improve your present position?" I was tasked and intrigued by his questions. At the same time, I was curious to know where he was going with this. *Could this actually be my interview? Could this be my moment in time that I have been so long waiting to have with this man at this company?* I was now beginning to get a little nervous. I felt my chest begin to tighten up, and the adrenaline flowing through my body now took on a whole new meaning of nervous. I needed to choose my words carefully before I answered Jonathan now because I am really being put on the spot.

Suddenly, Jonathan shifted gears on me. He asked me if I had any idea why he was flying to Boston in an emergency. I didn't know how to answer and just returned a blank stare to his expressionless eyes as he looked down at his fingers that appeared to be trembling. I felt like an absolute heel. Here I was so focused on myself that I didn't even think to ask why he had to leave his meeting in such an emergency. *This was all about me, wasn't it?* I apologized to Jonathan and asked him to forgive my inconsiderate attitude. I explained to him that I was just so overwhelmed in emotion about the interview that I didn't think to relate to him as just another human being wanted to share a few moments in the airport with another human being enjoying a friendly conversation.

This appeared to be all about me and my needs and my venue. How selfish of me! Jonathan looked back up at me and excused himself as he had to take a phone call that just came into his cell phone. Before I could respond, he was a hundred yards away from me near one of the concessions and appeared to be crying. Here I was watching a high-level executive of a multimillion-dollar organization breaking down and showing his human side to me. Without thinking, I ran to him and left both of our briefcases on the seats that we were sitting one hundred yards away. Jonathan immediately signaled me to stay where I was and to guard the briefcases that contained our laptops and started walking toward me, however, very slowly.

He shared with me that he just lost his sister, who was in a terrible car accident and in a coma. He wanted to see her alive one more time, but it wasn't meant to be. At that moment, I forgot the reason why I actually wanted to talk to Jonathan. For this moment in time, the human connection was much more important than the job. Our collective humanities, along with life's challenges, superseded our status and position in society. At this point, I realized why I was at this place in time, sharing this moment Jonathan. I made a connection with him that I could never, ever have accomplished during an interview. I just learned that true leadership has to do with people's emotional connections and not their professions. Jonathan realized that he could never catch another moment with his sister, where she could respond back to him and smile or frown, take his side, or disagree with him.

Jonathan looked up at me and stated, "Now you know why I was heading back to Boston in such an emergency." He sighed and then stated, "Now you also know why I had to put off your interview."

I remember putting my hands over my head leaning over and softly saying, "There is a reason for everything. I just learned a valuable lesson from us hooking up today." Jonathan said,

"Oh yeah, what was that?"

I looked at him nervously and said, "I believe I just made a lifelong friend, and that is more important to me than any interview anywhere, any time!" Jonathan looked up at me and smiled despite the tragic news he had just received.

He looked up at me, grabbed his itinerary, and said, "I know that you never made it to the interview. I also know that you were not in the bathroom when I walked through the reception area at 11:00 a.m." He looked at me in a very gentle and nonaggressive manner and said, "As soon as you called and stated that you are going to be late to my executive assistant, I took you off the interview list."

I looked at him quite startled and said to him in a very soft voice, "Then I will not be on the list to be called, despite the fact you had to leave for an emergency."

He said, "You got that right."

Speaking of being on an emotional roller coaster, it now feels like I am witnessing and out of body experience because I have just jumped out of my skin! Fate has taken a different turn with me right now, and I believe there was a reason for all this. I heard in the distance that Jonathan's flight number, 764, was beginning to board, and he was flying first class. He looks at his ticket and says to me, "I no longer have a reason to rush back to Boston now, do I?"

I looked at him in a very startling manner and abruptly stated, "I guess not."

Jonathan looked at me and said, "What time is your flight back to Boston?" I stated it wasn't until 8:30 p.m., Pacific time, and would not arrive in Boston until 5:00 a.m., Eastern Standard Time. He looked at me, his face grimaced, and he said, "Let's see if I can get my ticket changed to your flight at 8:30 p.m., and I will fly back with you to Boston." He also went on to tell me that he hadn't eaten in several hours and was famished and that he needed to get over the very emotional and disturbing news. He just received. He stated that he needed time to regroup his thoughts.

Here I was talking to a perfect stranger who I was going to interview with several hours ago. I missed the interview and was not scheduled for a reschedule of that interview and perhaps the chance of a lifetime to get a great job. I am in the middle of an airport with the guy I was supposed to interview with today who wanted to spend quality time with me on a later flight that he was not scheduled to take. He now wants to change his ticket, which will give us several hours to get something to eat and talk at dinner on the plane. My interview will not be a scheduled one-hour interview; it will actually be a conversation with another human being who will spend several hours learning about me, Josh Keating, the person, the man, the mentee of Jonathan Peters, whose last thought would be to experience an accidental interview, which would change his life forever and guide him to becoming a great leader.

LEADERSHIP LESSON

None of us is totally in control of ourselves at all times. At the beginning of this chapter, Josh is going through the gamut of emotions as his plans fell apart. Like most of us in these circumstances, he began to rationalize and grasp for a safe haven. Jonathan showed us that even a consummate professional is not immune from bursting into tears in public. Our emotions are an integral part of ourselves, and we cannot deny them.

In fact, emotions are a vital part of leadership. They allow us to show others that we truly care for them and inspire them to believe in us. The emotional connection is an essential part of building a team.

Part of this emotional connection is the willingness to be candid. A leader can't develop those he leads unless he can be honest about the areas where they need to change. Likewise, team members will not be receptive to criticism unless they trust that their leader is acting in their best interests. Jonathan doesn't tell Josh that he saw through his misleading statements about being present for the interview until after an emotional connection had been made. By changing his flight to the red-eye, he sent a clear signal that his goal was to help Josh grow.

All leaders need to be aware of the signals they send and how their actions affect trust. The unemotional facades we erect don't help us show that we care.

Chapter 3

THE AWAKENING

Making conversation is not always my strong suit. I would be spending the next several hours with the man who was supposed to interview me with no longer than one hour several hours ago. In addition, I would have been competing with several other candidates for a job I wanted very badly. I have been getting increasingly nervous about talking with him as I know very little about him, and he could potentially be my future boss. As Jonathan was trying to get his airplane ticket transferred to my flight, I was getting myself into a frenzy, wondering what I was going to say to him and wondering how to prevent myself from sticking my foot in my mouth when I talk to him. The waiting time for him to get his ticket changed seemed like an eternity. Finally, Jonathan came back with a smile on his face with a ticket for a seat on my flight in proximity to where I would be sitting. All he had to do was switch his seat with someone else on the flight so we could be next to each other and chat.

Jonathan sat down next to me in the waiting area and suggested we look for a restaurant near the airport where we could eat and learn a little bit more about each other. My nervousness started to ease up, and I began to be a little chattier. We found a restaurant about two hundred yards outside the airport. The name of the restaurant was Dream Pasta. I had never seen so much pasta in my entire life. There were so many different varieties of pasta that it would take me over two hours just to choose my selection. The restaurant was very elegant, and the prices were very expensive. I am not surprised considering that the restaurant was just outside the airport. Jonathan told me not to look at the prices and just order whatever I wanted. It was on him. I insisted on splitting the bill with him, and he just returned a cold stare back at me, and I got the message.

After we consumed hors d'oeuvres and a few drinks, Jonathan became very pensive while we were waiting for the main course to arrive. The silence was deafening, and the confusion in my head increased to a point where I was compelled to break the silence. It was like dead air on a phone conversation where nothing was said by either party for thirty seconds or more. Finally, I said to Jonathan, "I am very, very sorry for the loss of your sister." I told him that I could not even imagine what he was going through at this time mentally and emotionally. I asked him if he was really close with his sister. Jonathan looked at me very pensively and stated, "She was fourteen years older than me, and I was the youngest of six children. My mom died of cancer when I was eight years old. She basically was like my sister and my mother at the same time. I could never thank her"—and his voice was cracking as he spoke—"for what she did for me." Jonathan then excused himself and took a handkerchief out of his pocket to wipe a tear falling from his eye.

I don't know what compelled me to ask this question, but I thought I would ask it anyway. I asked Jonathan why he felt he could never thank his sister for what she did for him. He looked up at me and said, "Did you ever hold a sparrow in your hand and it could not fly?" I looked to Jonathan as if he had three heads. I thought he was losing his mind. He then said, "You then discover that the sparrow has a broken leg." I was looking at Jonathan intensely and looking for a punch line here. "You have to either make the choice to kill the sparrow and take it out of its misery, or you put a splint on its leg and nurse it back to health." I looked at Jonathan and was beginning to get the message. He was that broken sparrow after his mother passed away, and his sister put him on the track to his success. Jonathan said to me that his sister was his hero. She was mother, sister, friend, and spiritual guide until he got married and moved out of the house. He stated she was only fifty-eight years old at the time of her death just a few hours ago. This would make Jonathan forty-four years old now and in the prime of his career. I must admit that the pasta was delicious, but the conversation was very emotional. I have several more questions about his sister and wasn't sure whether or not he wants to answer them. Under the circumstances, he may shy away from discussing her since he just learned that she lost her life this very day. Jonathan stated he did want to talk about her as her memory is a tower of strength for him. She was his lifeline and his confidant in life. He stated that she would always offer him hope when he was down and feeling sorry for himself. Most of all, he made a strong point of stating that his sister never stopped believing in him, even when we stopped believing in himself.

He went onto say that life had no guarantees, no matter how strong the roadmap and how exact the details on the destinations. At this point, I was looking at Jonathan in a totally different light. This man was the real thing. He was a genuine human being whom I felt that I knew all my life and I knew that I physically have never met him before today. We were connected today because we were communicating with one another, not as manager to subordinate but collegially as one human being sharing his life with another human being in finding a common denominator of communication that puts us all in a comfort zone of knowledge acquisition. I looked at this conversation as a learning process of how one begins on the road to becoming an effective leader. Yes, it is true that Jonathan may have learned from his sister not only about life but about himself.

Jonathan, after losing his mother at such an early age and later learning from him that his father left his mother when he was only two years old, had only his sister to guide him as well as his other siblings on the road to success. However, I also later learned that only one other of his siblings, a third child, Michael, is now an executive with a well-known software company in the Midwest. The others are either in school or working at fast-food establishments. They all made choices in life, and Jonathan's sister, Patricia, the oldest sibling that started him on his career to success, encouraged all of her siblings to have passion for what they do best, and she will always love and respect them for it.

I just got finished eating a very delicious dinner and now feeling very relaxed. It almost appears as if I had known Jonathan for years, and I've only known him for a few hours. How can that be when I feel so comfortable with someone that I only knew a very short time? True relationships are built on trust. I remember that not too long ago, Jonathan trusted me with his briefcase while he went to the men's room. This made me realize in so many ways why he rose to the level that he did at such a very young age; I guess it all started with his sister, bringing him up without a mother or father and also taking care of her siblings. It often makes me think of what I've asked myself so many times. Are leaders are born or they are made? Here we were, Jonathan and myself, from two very different environments, coming together without plan or revocation, having a session where at this point in time we could've never found out about each other during a one-hour interview that could decide my working career for the rest of my life.

I am also realizing at this point that Jonathan had shared so much about himself with me, knowing very little, if any, information about my past or background. I didn't feel that he thought any information about me is irrelevant. It's only that he trusted me enough to share some very personal information about himself. Jonathan kept his promise and paid the bill after we ate. He wouldn't even let me leave the tip without drinks; the bill was over $125. He just smiled, put his wallet back in his pocket, and signaled me to the door. He excused himself while he received a call from his younger brother about what had happened to his sister. His brother seemed to be very shaken up, and Jonathan was vehemently trying to calm him down. Jonathan assured his brother that he would be arriving in Boston early tomorrow morning and would meet him there with his other siblings to make funeral arrangements. It was apparent, his sister was quite loved by his entire family, and I am not surprised.

It took us a couple of hours to eat dinner and chat, and it was actually getting close to boarding time for our flight to Boston. We sat in the waiting area of the airport terminal in silence. Jonathan appeared to be very melancholy and wrote many notes into his laptop while accepting calls from family members on his sister's death and people from work. I overheard him telling his executive assistant that he would be checking in with her in the middle of the week and use any resources that she needed in order to make the department run smoothly. It was apparent that he trusted her and knew she was capable of stepping in when he stepped out. I looked up at Jonathan after he got off the phone with his executive assistant whose name I later learned was Addy, short for Adeline. I inferred to Jonathan that she probably had been working for him for a very long time. He chuckled, looked up at me, and smiled and related to me that she had been working for him only about a year and a half, but she could do her job and his ten times better than him during the week and twice as good on weekends with her eyes closed. He revealed that she had twenty-two years as a high school principal under her belt when she retired, and he hired her full time. He sat back in his seat in a reclining position stretched widely and said, "I am going to close my eyes for ten minutes just to regroup."

I smiled back at him and said, "I think I'll join you. I just hope we don't miss the flight."

We did get our call to board the plane as scheduled, and neither one of us really got any shut-eye. Both of us had too much on our minds to shut our brains off. I think we were both anxious to get home and face our challenges in our respective worlds. Despite the fact that my brain wouldn't shut off, my body was very fatigued and, at the same time, very relaxed. From personal experience when that happens, your body does not tighten up from the stress normally produced by your thoughts, no matter how much your brain tries to stress your body. As a result, your mind produces data more succinctly and in clearer patterns that you ever thought possible. You begin to process information in gradient levels that translate themselves into clear, uninhibited verbiage that draws no boundaries and accepts all opportunities. In other words, you have reached that aha moment that makes your life begin to make sense with your career choices, and you know that the shoe fits.

It was now 8:20 p.m., and we were safely boarded on the plane. It was a full flight, and we were on time to take off at 8:30 p.m. No matter how hard I tried to make myself comfortable on the plane, my mind could not shut off. I kept thinking of all the things that had just transpired in the past twelve hours in my life. In a moment of deep thoughts, just after we took off and were in safe sky space, Jonathan asked me if I wanted a drink. I said, "No, thank you. However, I would like for us to continue our conversation where we left off at the restaurant."

Jonathan looked at me in a very pensive manner, then asked me, "Do you always like to be in control?" I was stunned by the tone and manner of his question. I did not know how to respond, and I was filled with mixed emotions.

I stuttered a response back to him almost immediately stating, "No! What do you mean?" I stated to Jonathan that I was not trying to be disrespectful or controlling. I told him that I was only trying to pick up where we left off because I thought the conversation was so interesting between us.

He looked at me in a very subtle and fatigued manner and said, "I am much too tired to deal with the BS." I was stunned by his comments and, quite frankly, offended.

"I am not sure what you mean, Jonathan, as I am fatigued as well!"

He then said to me, "I wasn't being personal, just factual." I looked at him intensely.

He went on to state, "What if I wasn't in the mood to talk? Would you then consider that you might be putting me on the spot, and I would be compelled to give you an answer?" Boy, did I feel stupid. I put my head down and didn't answer him.

"You know something, Josh. I am really sorry for coming down on you so hard. I really didn't mean to offend you. I have my moments as well when I appear to be in everybody's face and don't even realize it. You remind me a lot of me when I was your age," Jonathan stated. "I used to think that the whole world was against me, and I had to somehow prove myself to show them that they were wrong."

Jonathan then asked me, "Do you think there is some divine plan in the karma that we ended up on this flight together?"

I looked at Jonathan and asked, "What do you mean, Jonathan?"

Well, Jonathan stated, "You were here to see me on an interview, and it never got to happen, and here I am speaking with you one-on-one on a six-and-a-half-hour flight back to Boston, giving you exclusivity for a personal interview." I looked at Jonathan, and I chuckled when I was starting to really get awake now. I actually now have the opportunity to talk to a man whom I arranged to have an interview a few hours back who would not have given me more than twenty minutes of his time when over fifty candidates (quarter finalists by the way) applying for this job would have killed to have this opportunity to talk to the CEO of Medical Solutions one-on-one.

I looked at Jonathan with utmost humility and said, "I don't really believe in karma. I do believe that it is a coincidence that some events occur and could be in your best interests." Jonathan looked at me in a very puzzled manner and then looked out the window and just stared out into space.

Jonathan then said to me, "I told you the story about my sister and what she meant to me. Did you have anybody in your life that helped you along the way?"

I looked at Jonathan as if to say, "Are we getting a little personal here?" However, something compelled me to answer his question. I remember putting my head down and almost talking into my hands, observing the indentations between my fingers, and then looking up to Jonathan and saying, "I was adopted, Jonathan. I was abandoned by my birthparents and placed in an orphanage in Boston called the Home for Little Wanderers." Jonathan listened intently. I went on to state, "They took very good care of me until I was eighteen years old, and then I was on my own. I put myself through school, lived on my own, and never got in trouble with the law." Jonathan looked at me as if to say go on. However, I could feel my body stirring with emotion, and a hidden resentment for my birthparents began to take me over, and I could feel my attitude changing rapidly.

Jonathan then said to me, "We can drop this conversation and get some rest if you wish. I feel like I've already crossed the line with you."

I remember lunging back at Jonathan and saying to him, "You, you, you are the only one that I have ever shared this with, and I don't know why." Jonathan was stunned.

He said, "You really don't have to talk about this!"

I remember lunging back at Jonathan and saying to him, "Yes, I do." I went on to state that when I applied for the job at Medical Solutions. I told them that my parents were dead. I never really explained anything to them. Somehow, I felt I needed to be brutally honest with Jonathan and break up some deep-seated emotions that I haven't felt since I was eighteen years old. There was something about him that made me feel like I wanted to tell someone the truth about me. Over the years, I have been to so many therapists and counselors because since I was given up by my birthparents; I always felt this huge hole in my heart and abandoned by the world. I had never really come to grips with this. Somehow, someway, I trusted Jonathan. Perhaps this was in the karma that I was sitting next to him on the plane to Boston. Maybe our time together on the plane was meant to be a lot more than just a job interview. Maybe, this is about trust and connecting with people.

Somehow, someway, I was realizing that I was learning a lot more about myself just by sitting next to Jonathan on an airplane. It appears that Jonathan could be a perfect mentor to me because he is making a connection with me like no one had ever done before. Even people closest to me in my life could not reach me like Jonathan did in the few hours that I have known him. This is insane. Is there some higher power that is controlling what's going on between us? I have to stop thinking like this as I am a realist and a pragmatist. I lived in the streets. Most of my life, I brought myself up and took some really hard knocks. I am twenty-nine years old, not in a relationship, and put myself through undergrad and graduate school and owe nobody anything in this world. I am my own person.

I looked over at Jonathan who appears to have dozed off. He had shades over his eyes, and I was sitting in the window seat and began looking out the window. Suddenly, I heard the sound of somebody moaning. Instinctively, I looked over at Jonathan, and there were tears coming down his cheeks under his eyeshades. I gently asked him if he was okay, and he nodded his head affirmatively. I began to look back out the window, and I heard Jonathan say to me, in a very low almost gravel-type voice, "Did you ever get a calling and not respond to the call?"

I looked at Jonathan. *Is it to say I don't know what you mean?* Jonathan took his eyeshades off and wiped his eyes with his handkerchief.

He cleared his throat and said while looking me right in the eyes, "I promised my sister before she died that I would help people who needed my help as she has helped me when I needed hers." I don't know what got into me, but I asked Jonathan why he was bringing this up now with me. At first, he didn't answer. Then he said, "Josh, you need to help yourself before you can help others."

Now, I was beginning to think that Jonathan was off his rocker. But then in an instant, I figured he was sharing with me something that he's never shared with anyone before now. I just did the same thing. I was making a people connection. Somehow, Jonathan and I developed a bond of trust. Here was an individual who was clearly in a very high profile leadership position. Here I was, just on an interview for a job with this high-profile person who is somehow sitting in a plane next to on my way home, mind you, after a failed interview attempt. This whole thing was insane. Was it just a coincidence? Or was it somehow part of the bigger plan, which put the two of us together? I looked at Jonathan, and I said, "Jonathan, perhaps I can help you if you help me so that I can help others."

Now it was all beginning to make sense to me. This plane ride was not about Jonathan or about me. This plane ride was about how Jonathan and I can help each other so that we could help others achieve their goals and follow their dreams. I felt that from this point on, he would be my mentor, and in many ways, I could be his, whether we worked together on not. We needed to find ourselves so we could lead and follow and follow and lead.

LEADERSHIP LESSONS

Why was Josh so offended when Jonathan raised the issue of control? As we progress through school, out beginning jobs, and first supervisory positions, we were rewarded for always being in control. Our grades in school and our advancement early in our careers come from our mastery of facts and awareness of details. However, as we move higher in organizations, the desire to be in control of situations becomes a limiting factor; no one had enough time to be on top of every detail as their responsibilities increase. Instead, we need to learn how to trust.

This is not blind trust but a confidence that objectives will be met if employees are carefully selected and developed, that objectives and limits are clearly stated, and that doors of communication are always open.

When we have shown that we trust others, they begin to trust us. Here Josh opened up to Jonathan in a way he never had before. This mutual trust carries over into the workplace, where Josh would trust enough to report issues, problems, and opportunities instead of editing reports to avoid personal consequences.

A true leader can rise to greater responsibility by setting the direction for the organization and letting others make the day-to-day decisions for their area. The leader still kept his finger on the pulse of the organization but at increasingly higher levels as employees rise to the occasion. A micromanager will always be limited to an area of responsibility he can control directly.

Chapter 4

THE MORNING AFTER THE DAY BEFORE

I finally arrived at my apartment Saturday afternoon about 1:00 p.m. After looking through my mail, unpacking my light luggage, feeding my cats, Molly and James, and grabbing something out of the fridge to eat, I kept thinking about what Jonathan said about me that I always wanted to be in control. I really never thought of myself that way. I always thought of myself as someone who was very subservient and took direction rather than give it except when dealing with my subordinates. I always thought of myself as rather easygoing rather than a control freak.

I know that I am going to have to face Lynn on Monday morning bright and early. I really dread that happening because I know that she will soon realize that I was supposed to be working on Friday and not at an airport in LAX. Yes, I will have many challenges on Monday. I don't know what I am going to say to Lynn. *How am I going to justify my absence? What will she be thinking?*

I really don't know very much about Lynn as she had only been my boss for a few months. I know that her predecessor was a tyrant who demanded much, gave little direction, and, when things went wrong, always put the blame on somebody else. Yes, let me tell you about Mike Feeney, the boss I had been working with for four and a half years before Lynn came on board. The man made me miserable and was one of the reasons why I wanted to leave my present place of employment. I guess I have been judging Lynn unfairly, putting her into a mold that stereotypes my previous boss. Feeney would never allow me to do anything on my own. Although I had six direct reports, Feeney would always be checking my work. He wouldn't even let me send a memo to any of my direct reports, unless he saw it first. You might say, he was a control freak!

I can't believe what I was just thinking. Could I be following in my predecessor's footsteps? This is a really scary thought. Could it be that Mike Feeney has rubbed off on me? Subconsciously, I am acting like him, and Jonathan picked up on it. I'll bet you. That's what it is. In the furthest realm of my imagination, I would never think I was anything like Mike Feeney.

Mike Feeney was a fifty-eight-year-old man who was always feared in my department. He never talked very much but always had an angry look on his face. He never seemed happy about anything. When you asked him a question, he would either been looking at the computer screen or writing something down. He would never look you in the eye. This would indicate that you were interrupting him and what you had to say was less important than what he was doing.

Whenever he would talk to you, Mike Feeney would always find the negatives in what you were saying. He would never tell you that you were doing a good job. He would always remind you that he was the boss and made you believe by the atmosphere he created that he could fire you at any time. I can't believe that this behavior rubbed off on me, and Jonathan saw right through that. I don't think I gave him any indication that I was rude, inconsiderate, and uncaring at any time yet picked up on control in my personality somehow.

Thinking like this is creating a lot of anxiety for me, I felt my body beginning to get tenses, and I was developing a massive headache. I haven't slept nights in almost thirty-six hours, and I felt like I could take a long nap. I remember falling asleep on the couch and abruptly waking up at about four o'clock after being in a deep sleep. I was startled by this loud banging on my door. I walked to the door, half awake and half asleep. I opened the door of my three-bedroom apartment, and there was a little boy no more than four or five years old, accompanied by an elderly gentleman who looked to be in his early seventies. The gentleman had a glazed look in his eyes and was smiling at me. He didn't say anything, just stared at me with a faraway look. The little boy looked at me and said, "Grandpa is lost." His voice was high and shrilling. The little boy appeared to be frightened. My first impulse was to dial 911 and call the police. I hesitated for a moment and wanted to ask my visitors some questions. However, under the circumstances, I needed to get them help right away. I asked the elderly gentleman if he had any form of identification. Both the child and the elderly gentleman continued to look at me and smiled. The elderly gentleman did not verbally respond.

After I dialed 911, the police finally arrived in less than ten minutes. They asked me what had happened, and I explained to them that the elderly gentleman and the little boy were banging on my door. I opened the door, and there they were. The police took down all the information and took the child with the elderly gentleman with them in the police cruiser. Twenty minutes later, they returned to my apartment and advised me that the gentleman with the child was an Alzheimer's patient living with his daughter and son-in-law. The police told me that they got the call from the elderly gentleman's daughter that he was missing with his six-year-old grandson, Peter, about ten minutes before I called. Apparently, his daughter was on the second floor of their house putting something in Peter's bedroom when the child and her father decided to walk out the door. She said she was only in his bedroom for two minutes and rarely left them alone out of her sight. The police thanked me and told me they would contact me if they needed anything else.

I was so worked up by this incident, I totally forgot about going back to work on Monday and what had just transpired over the weekend. It was interesting that what took precedence were the unexpected events that just took place with the young boy and his grandfather. It started to make me think a little bit about control and myself. I was feeling so many conflicting emotions at this point that I was immersed with anxiety. I wasn't sure about who I was as a human being, more than what role I played at work. Could it be that I was seeking to control others because I didn't have control of myself. In other words, I wasn't sure if being me was good enough to work in my own role, and I hid my insecurity by attempting to control the behavior of others. I remembered that I studied this stuff in a graduate class I took in psychology. I believe they referred to this as pseudoepistemology, a false ego.

It really scared me to think that I no longer was the person I thought I was and felt even more inferior. I was even apprehensive about going to work on Monday. I decided to order some pizza and relax a bit. I wanted to forget things for a while and maybe even hook up with some friends over the weekend. I began feeling more and more anxious and wanted to jump out of my skin. Nothing could relax me. My chest began to tighten. I felt shortness of breath. I thought I was having a heart attack, and I even considered going to the emergency room. Suddenly, that same feeling that gave me the adrenaline I needed at the airport to talk to Jonathan took control over me. I suddenly became calm and focused. I realized that the events at the airport were not within my control. The unplanned confrontation with Lynn and the unplanned meeting with Jonathan were not within my control. The only thing within my control was my trip to LA.

My question is at this point, why do I have a need to control when most events that occur are not within my control except the ones that I plan myself? I now began to realize that I have turned into Mike Feeney although I despised him so much and could not wait until the day that he would move on, which he did. Yes, he was my role model. I always felt he was the most despicable human being on the planet. However, in hindsight, I always felt he was a great manager. He ruled by fear and intimidation, and he did this with a smile. His goal was to always make sure that his department did everything perfection because "his people's," as he said, performance reflected on him.

A typical meeting or briefing, as he would call it, consisted of me putting together every single line item I worked on with my team the previous day. He would always say you are not working them hard enough. He would tell me I needed to constantly check their work if he was to get his reports correctly done. I would always walk out of that morning meeting with strong feelings of animosity toward Mike. I realized now that when I walked out of that meeting with Mike, I was acting as an extension of his arm.

I remembered walking out of Mike's office in going into my own morning meeting with my pool of six employees and telling them that they could not send out any work unless I personally looked at and approved the work. When my crew made suggestions, I would always shoot them down and tell them they needed to do the work the way I just explained it to them. My crew would always have a dejected look on their faces. Often, they would try to tell me that they didn't agree with something I told them to do. I would just reiterate that they do it my way, and I was responsible for their work.

I know that in the past week I lost two of my crew to the competitive companies that don't even pay as well as we do here. I needed to hire two employees right away, and they were not my best choices. However, under the pressure of satisfying clients' needs, I needed to make the hires right away. After Mike had his heart attack and his doctors advised him that he transfer to a less stressful location, they hired Lynn, my present supervisor. Although I felt I deserved the job and this is why I am presently interviewing for another job, they hired Lynn, the external candidate, over me. I thought that this was totally unfair. *I deserved that job. I have been working at this company for over five years and more than proved myself here. Why didn't they see that? What is it that they saw in her and didn't see in me?* Well, now she is my boss, and there is nothing I can do about it.

As I continued to contemplate about my meeting with Lynn on Monday, this rush went through my body. However, the adrenaline flowed, but in a good way. Lynn did not question my judgment on candidates I had chosen to replace the employees that have moved on to other companies. She told me that the goal should be to keep the organization and our department running smoothly. This makes her much different than Mike Feeney, now doesn't it?

Perhaps it won't be so bad meeting with Lynn after all. Let's see what happens in their meeting on Monday and chapter 5.

LEADERSHIP LESSONS

Learning to lead is a lifelong process, and we learn from both the good and bad attributes of those who play an important role for us. Without realizing it, Josh had taken on Mike's controlling style. This emulation of his boss is so ingrained that he doesn't see the negative impacts it is having on his performance. The loss of two employees should have been a clear sign, but Josh can only think of the effect of their departure on his workload.

As a potential leader, we need to be very careful whom we choose for a role model. Mike may be in a position of authority, but that doesn't make him a leader. We can show him the respect due his position without allowing him to affect our core attitudes.

As a leader, we need to be careful in the messages we send. We all have good days and bad, times when we are able to connect on a personal level, and times when the pressure of the moment short-circuits our best intentions. Harkening back to chapter 1, we have to maintain self-control if we are going to serve as effective role models.

We also needed to observe the effect our behavior was having on those who looked up to us. There was always a temptation to attribute other's actions to their skills rather than reflecting on whether it might be a reaction to something we did or said.

Chapter 5

TIME TO FACE THE MUSIC

I chilled out most of Sunday and met up with some friends and truly relaxed. I really didn't give much thought Monday at all until I got home about 9:00 p.m. I must admit that most of Sunday was concentrating on the things that I value most in my life. I value my parents, my friends, and, believe it or not, my relationship with the fish in my goldfish tank. I don't know what it's like to be married or have children. I am twenty-eight years old and not in a serious relationship with anyone. I broke up with my girlfriend about six months ago because she would not give me the time I needed to build a serious relationship. You might say that Maggie was a workaholic. She was thirty-two years old, a single mom divorced last year, and a certified public accountant with her own practice. Come to think of it, Maggie always stated that I was much too passive; I needed to be more aggressive in my decisions personally and professionally.

I woke up Monday, the last Monday of April, and the birds were singing, it was fifty-two degrees, and the air was so fresh. It was 6:30 a.m., and the sun was actually out shining through my kitchen window onto my refrigerator. I went outside to get the *Wall Street Journal*, which I have delivered to my home Monday through Friday. As I stooped down to get my newspaper while smelling fresh spring air, I noticed that my rosebushes were starting to come up through the ground and would eventually end up in a few short weeks as beautiful pink, yellow, and red roses. I asked myself, *How do these roses know that they need to come up through the ground? How do they know the change in the seasons?* I rationalized that they don't have a brain like we do. They don't have fancy calendars. They don't have memorandums. They don't get warnings if they don't come up on time. They just know what to do, and when to do it. They are not micromanaged but do follow a strategic plan. They exist and serve a purpose.

Somehow, these roses fit into the big puzzle that is, by design, a component of the universe that makes everything in that universe somehow function in harmonious and methodical sequence without being reminded why they exist. It is just that they do exist to serve a purpose, and when that purpose ends, they move on. If there is such a thing, I am thinking "senseless sense."

I now begin to get dressed. After taking a shower, eating my breakfast, and reading my *Wall Street Journal*; I begin thinking about what I'm going to say to Lynn when I get into work. As I stated earlier, Lynn started with us a few months ago. Although I was not one of the finalists, when Mike Feeney's job opened up, I still thought I had every qualification to take Mike's position and bring the department to new levels. Perhaps that didn't come across in the interview when I had my meeting with the chief financial officer and the CEO of our company. Lynn started her first day on February 15, 2013, after six months of interviewing candidates for Mike's job. The job boiled down to her. Lynn is an attractive woman, dresses very professionally, and has a really warm personality. She is someone you would probably love to have as a neighbor next door. She is my boss and not my neighbor, and I have to keep that in mind.

When Lynn started working for Biotech Medical on February 15, she immediately met with all of her direct reports and brought us into a conference room. She told us everything about her. She was thirty-eight years old, a single mother of two, a graduate of Babson College with an MBA in corporate finance. She was with her last company located in Wisconsin for eleven years until the company was sold and moved overseas. She did not choose to relocate with her two children and preferred to remain in the United States. The previous position she held was manager of corporate finance at a Fortune 500 company. She saw this opportunity at Biotech Medical as a wonderful way to prove her leadership skills as director of operations in a major city like Boston. She had tremendous financial experience in a global setting, and Biotech Medical thought she would be the best choice to replace Mike.

Lynn told us that her management style was more laissez-faire van than directive or, as she put it, punitive. She believes that everyone in her department had something to offer and was a valuable asset to the organization. Her role was how to develop us rather than how to get rid of us, so she said, "No worries." She was determined to work with us and to bring out the best in every one of us. She emphasized that she had an open-door policy and that we could ask her anything, no matter how ridiculous we thought it was, she would be there to assist. I believe that set us off on the right foot and gave us some inkling of the type of a boss that she would be. So why was I so apprehensive in meeting with her this morning? Was it because of my own guilt? In fact, what do I have to be guilty of? Everyone from time to time goes on an interview and can tell their boss about it.

I just scared myself listening to myself, if that is possible. I am trying to create values on a paradigm that I have learned in my years of working for Mike Feeney. Let me explain. I am trying to justify an ethical value with a business decision. My business decision was to look at other prospects outside of my present place of employment. My next question is, am I leaving because I am not happy with the company's decision to hire someone other than myself for the director of operations position? Or is my business decision about my not being challenged enough at my present position that I have to move on to something else? I think that I need to answer these questions first, before I meet with Lynn.

Looking at this dilemma from an ethical perspective is really not germane to why I was at LAX last Friday. What is germane is whether or not my emotions to interview elsewhere had anything to do with my position at my company and my relationship with my present boss. I really didn't know enough about Lynn to judge or decide whether or not I waned to work for her. I really haven't honestly assessed my job at Biotech to see whether or not I could grow in that position with a new boss at the helm. I was basing my decision to leave Biotech on my relationship with Feeney and not my relationship with Biotech. My question now is, when I walk into work, will I be looking at Mike Feeney when I address why I was at LAX last Friday and not at Biotech? Or will I be addressing Lynn? I need to put all of this in perspective and rationalize—this is my problem and not Lynn's problem. I can't go into the meeting with her, attacking her about something that she had no part of in any way shape or form. She expected me to be into work last Friday and saw me somewhere else.

I am a little curious as to why she didn't ask me when she saw me at LAX why I wasn't at Biotech. Does this say something about her as a leader? Yes, it does appear that I have somehow turned into a Mike Feeney. You see, Mike Feeney didn't trust anyone, perhaps not even himself. He was always skeptical when somebody ran something by his very limited attention span to the needs of others. He was basically always looking to cover his own interests and his own domain and make sure that nothing penetrated the fortress that he built over the years. Could it be that Lynn actually trusted me and that be the reason why she didn't ask me any questions as to why I wasn't at work." What if I had a family emergency? What if there was something going on in my life, for example, a medical test that I needed to address at a hospital on the West Coast or suddenly called away to attend to the needs of a close family member? In essence, I created my own skepticism of how I would look at the situation if I were Lynn based on Mike Feeney's values. These thoughts are really scaring me and now making me realize my effectiveness as a leader. I am realizing that if I can't lead my own values, trust in my own emotions, and give others the opportunity to rationalize their motives and not mine, I am a mediocre manager and a very poor leader.

I drive a 2010 BMW 325 convertible, which I lease at $550 per month and don't have a problem making the payments. My present salary is $62,000 a year with an up to 10 percent bonus incentive based on corporate earnings. I also have a generous 401(K) retirement plan with company match of 6 percent before taxes on my contributions. My health care is paid at 80 percent, and I get four weeks vacation per year and twelve sick days. If I got the director's position that Lynn now holds, the starting salary would be 95K with slightly better incentives and profit sharing. Also, I would get a company car.

It is now 8:15 a.m., Monday, April 29, and I am on my way to work. As I said, the sun is shining beautifully, and I am trying to think pleasant thoughts. However, the only thought that was going through my mind was what I was going to say to Lynn when she asked me about Friday. I couldn't help it. I am conditioned that way. I needed to get a grip on myself and only focus on coming into work and what I needed to do since I have left the office last Thursday. I am only about a half-hour from work, and I walk in the door, and everyone, including the receptionist, is very cheerful. All of them are singing "Happy Monday." This puts a nice feeling through my body until I arrive at my office. I opened the door to my office, and I observed stacks of boxes on my desk, on the floor, and some piled in my office chair. The adrenaline immediately began to flow through my body, and I gasped in horror and amazement. I still had my briefcase in my hand when Lynn's executive assistant smiled at me and escorted me to the conference room.

I felt for sure that this was it. I was going to be fired. I was waiting for Lynn to come into the conference room at any minute. I was escorted into the conference room at 8:55 a.m., and it was 9:20 a.m., and I was still sitting there by myself. It felt like an eternity. I wanted to jump out of my skin. I wanted to just walk out of the building and never look back. After all the time and effort I put into the company, this is what they do. This is how they pay me back. Well, I will not give them the opportunity to fire me. I will just quit before the words come out of their mouth. How dare she jump to conclusions without knowing the facts! Finally, at 9:25 a.m., Russell Hampton, chief operating officer of Biotech stepped into the conference room with Lynn's assistant. He asked me if I wanted a cup of coffee or anything to eat before he got started. I said no thank you to him and was looking around for Lynn to enter the conference room. I didn't see her anywhere.

Russell asked me if I was comfortable and then stated he had some news to share with me. Lynn's assistant then left the conference room and closed the door. I was alone with Russell. He didn't say anything for about ten seconds, which seemed like an eternity. He was staring at his folded hands and suddenly looked up at me and said, "Okay, Josh, let's begin our discussion." Saturday evening at about 8:30 p.m. I got a call from Lynn Ann Marconi who stated to me in a very calm voice that she has accepted another position with a Biotech firm in Los Angeles, California. She is very sorry that she is not able to give me more notice to train someone else for her position at Biotech. She explained to me that the opportunity came very suddenly and that her accepting the position was contingent upon the fact that she starts immediately based on financial circumstances at the company that she could not disclose with me. Lynn told me she was very sorry but could not give up the opportunity. Russell told me he was startled by it and had no choice but to accept the resignation and immediately start a search for a new director of operations. Since I was her closest direct report, he asked me if I would be kind enough to fill in her position in the interim until he was able to hire a replacement. He told me I would be given serious consideration as her replacement, and this would be a perfect opportunity for me to prove myself while he was interviewing for her replacement. Over the next six months, I asked why six months? He stated that these positions take at least that long to find the right person. He stressed to me that he would be focused in more than just the recruitment and selection end of this position but also the retention end. He did not want to waste time, money, and energy in recruiting another Lynn fiasco.

 Russell stated to me that the choice was mine. However, he would strongly recommend I consider my options at Biotech. He stated again that this was a perfect opportunity for me to prove myself. Maybe I could be that leader. Maybe I could capitalize on my strengths and not feel sorry for myself about my deficiencies. Maybe I could be something better than Mike Feeney and even Lynn, whom I never really got to know. Most importantly, I could develop into the me that I really never got to know until now. Maybe, just maybe, I might be lucky enough to find a mentor or have a mentor find me and help me climb that corporate ladder. You know, it just dawned on me why Lynn never asked me why I was at LAX! Perhaps she thought I might ask the same question of her. Little did I know she was meeting her future boss who never showed up at the airport as planned but contacted her later to finalize her employment decision. It was all in the karma.

LEADERSHIP LESSONS

Josh's thought about capitalizing on his strengths rather than his deficiencies is a major leap in his path to leadership. None of us is without deficiencies; a true leader will readily admit them. Only by accepting his areas of weakness can he build a team that will fill the gaps and achieve his objectives.

Josh was looking for a mentor, but his search needs to be deeper than simply an advisor more experienced than he is—a leader more than just a mentor. His primary objective is to achieve his organization's goals. In order to do this, he must develop the skills of others, deploy his resources effectively, and inspire his team. One of the outcomes of mentoring is that people are better able to move up the corporate ladder, but this happens because of the development of their technical, managerial, and leadership skills. The leader also provides developmental opportunities and guidance; the team member must still prove their ability to handle the next level of responsibility.

As we saw earlier, Jonathan had accomplished this by building a relationship with Josh based on mutual trust. As a team, they can achieve great things for their organization.

Chapter 6

LOST IN TRANSLATION

The first words out of my mouth that were directed to Russell was, "Why is all my stuff packed in boxes in my office?"

Russell said, "Excuse me?"

I repeated my question, "Why is all my stuff packed in boxes if I am not fired?"

Russell said, "Who said anything about you being fired?"

My initial response was, "What would you think if you saw all your stuff packed in boxes?"

Russell didn't say anything to me. He just looked at me with a blank stare, chuckled, and said, "A picture is not always worth a thousand words."

"What you see packed in these boxes is Lynn's belongings and work since she started here a few months ago."

I immediately panicked and said to Russell, "Where is all my stuff then?"

He answered, "In the boxes mixed with Lynn's stuff."

This was not making any sense to me. I immediately snapped back at Russell and asked, "How did you know I was going to take her job over unless you talked to me first?" Russell then took me out of the conference room and brought me to his office. He asked me to close the door.

"Josh," he said. "I have been watching you for some time now. Especially in the past year, you have shown a lot of potential, but not a lot of promise. I knew that you were disgruntled, and my hands were tied at the time." Russell told me that Mike Feeney has been having cardiac issues for some time now and discussed with him that he was getting near retirement and asked me to put a severance package together for him. Russell told me that Mike was a great manager but did not have the ability to bring the department forward. He told me that Mike Feeney had no vision or innovation.

About three months before Mike Feeney retired, Russell told me that he was going over my review with Mike. Mike stated that I had no innovation or creativity. He also told Russell that I wasn't really effective in my job as a financial account manager and that he spent most of his time correcting my mistakes. He told me that I really didn't know how to lead my subordinates and recommended that a replacement be found for me before he retires. I was sitting in awe with my mouth open when Russell was telling me all this. I could not believe my ears. Russell then looked at me and stated, "You see that you are still here. This should say something about my judgment." Russell told me that he told Mike he would take all of his advice under advisement, and he would let Mike know his decision on the next plan of action of leadership in my department.

Russell told me that two weeks later he called Mike into his office and told him that he decided to hire a replacement for him and not to let me go, despite his recommendation. Although Mike was not happy with Russell's decision, he was a loyal employee and trusted Russell's judgment. Russell went on to explain that three weeks before Mike left the company, he decided to hire a young lady to replace him by the name of Lynn Anne Marconi. He told me that Lynn Anne was well-versed in the biotech field and had several years of international finance experience working at a company on the West Coast. He later stated that the company she worked for is a well-known giant in the industry and goes under the name of Medical Solution Inc.

I sat in my chair in Russell's office with my mouth wide open and frozen from my head to my toes. I could not move based on the information that I just heard. Russell told me not to look so surprised and that he had known I had applied to Medical Solutions, right after he decided to hire Lynn for Mike Feeney's position. Russell further explained to me that Lynn was only a loaner from Medical Solutions until he could hire someone to do Mike's job. Russell chuckled and said to me, "Don't look so surprised." He said, "Jonathan Peters and I have been friends for many years. We grew up together in Boston."

I said, "You've got to be kidding me. Tell me this is all a joke!" Russell told me that he decided to stay in Boston and seek employment in biotech companies. Jonathan decided to go to the West Coast, where he thought there would be more opportunity. He went on to say that he and Jonathan were still very good friends. Therefore, when Mike Feeney left and Russell knew it would take a long time to find a replacement for him, he was going to look at internal and external candidates for the job. However, in the biotech world, one could never sit on your finances since most of the funding is utilized toward research and development. Liquidity is essential for research. Jonathan then agreed to loan me Lynn Anne Marconi until I could find a suitable replacement for Mike.

Russell told me that he didn't know very much about Lynn. Therefore, although he trusted Jonathan, he had a fiduciary responsibility to answer to his shareholders about anyone holding a key management position in the company despite the position would only be available for a few months until he found a replacement for Mike. Now all this was beginning to make sense to me, and it was getting very scary, but in a good way. I was now starting to see the bigger picture, and I wasn't sure emotionally how I could handle all this. This was like being on a giant roller coaster. And I just got to the top of the highest jump, and now I was going to go down the deepest slope. My question is, am I ready for this next step? Well, one thing I do know is that leadership is about taking risks. However, in this case, I had no control over this risk I was about to take. So my question is, "Is this really a risk or is it a challenge?"

Russell went on to explain to me that when it was time for Jonathan to take her back to Medical Solutions, Jonathan wanted to find out about her accomplishments at Biotech, which included getting information about her direct reports while she was there. He explained to me that my name came up as one of her direct reports and that she was very impressed with my abilities and innovations but was concerned about me for validation on every task I performed from her. She said that I had a fear that if I were not in control of everything I did at all times, I would lose my job. She pegged me as a control freak. Again, my heart was in my mouth, and I was frozen from the head to the feet. This is all starting to unfold now. I now realize that Lynn knew I was going on the interview with Jonathan, even to the date and time. Jonathan knew I was coming in that day to meet him. Then my question is, "Why all the charades? Why didn't they just tell me they all knew what was going on and what I was up to?"

Russell asked me at this point, while in my frozen state, if I wanted a glass of water or a cup of coffee. I told him I was fine and that I found what he had to say very interesting and intriguing. Now it is all beginning to make sense to me. Jonathan knew absolutely nothing about my ability to be able to communicate on a more human level than just being a paper pusher. Mike Feeney would never allow me to come out of my shell and show the human side of me, and this is what Lynn had to learn about me at Russell's request, as a favor from Jonathan. Russell went on to explain to me that despite what Mike Feeney said about me, he had been evaluating me for quite some time as Mike's replacement. However, he never had proof whether or not I was capable of bringing Mike's department to the next level.

Lynn had a much different leadership style. She was not laissez-faire, nor was she transformational. In retrospect, I found her leadership to be charismatic, which is what you need when you are looking for organizational change. You need to be passionate about what you do, but you also had to be motivational. Individuals must believe that you can take them to where they want to go, rather than where you think they need to go to be successful. It is now apparent to me that Lynn's job was to take me out of my shell and prove to Russell as a favor from Jonathan whether or not I would be able to bring the finance department to where it needed to be in order to raise funding for biotechnical research. Russell also told me that Medical Solutions did not want to lose me, and after several months of interviewing external candidates at Mike Feeney's request, they could not find one individual that could be groomed to do the job that represented the next evolution for fundraising in our company.

Russell then went on to explain to me that over the next six months, Jonathan, Lynn, and him would mentor, coach, and assist me in getting the job, I so desperately thought I deserved. Biotech's board still will want to review and continue interviewing for external candidates. However, Russell told me the decision would be his in the end. At this point, I was filled with all types of emotions, and I didn't know whether to laugh, cry, jump out of my skin strangled the living daylights out of Russell for playing with my emotions, or just say thank you. I think I'll go with the thank you.

Finally, I asked Russell if Jonathan really had a sister that passed away. Russell looked up at me and said, "What matters is that you two connected and for all the right reasons." I got up, shook Russell's hand, left his office, and started unpacking all of the material I would need for the next six months. In my old office.

LEADERSHIP LESSONS

Russell has taken advantage of Mike's retirement to construct a situation where he can observe Josh in a variety of circumstances and assess his potential for leadership. Too many of us put people in slots based on superficial appearances and an aura of professionalism. Too often we are surprised when these impressions turn out to be wrong, and our organizations suffer for our error.

Each of us has roles in which we can be very effective and roles where we are less effective (possibly even disruptive). If an organization is to meet its objectives, the leader must have a very good idea how people will act (and react). This allows him to assign roles where each individual is most effective. Whenever possible, a leader adapts the role to the employee's skills and style, emphasizing developmental opportunities.

If this seems like a lot of work for the leader, think about the consequences of assigning someone to a role that is not appropriate for them. If we're lucky, the result is only mediocre performance. In the worst case, an employee's response in a minor emergency can turn the situation into a full-blown catastrophe. Inevitably, the public assigns responsibility to the individuals involved, but the real blame should fall to the manager who put the employee in a position he was unprepared for on an emotional level.

Chapter 7

FINDING THE ANSWERS

I look at my watch, and it is now about 10:30 a.m. on Monday, May 6, 2013. It seemed like an eternity sitting in Russell's office. All this time I thought I was getting fired when in reality I was getting sort of a promotion. I have so many mixed emotions going through my head right now that I don't know whether to go left to right, up or down, or just walk out of the company. That anxious feeling is coming back again, and I had to make it stop. I had to tell myself I was in control but for the right reasons. I am the master of my own destiny, and I create my own demons of my choosing. We need to do this one step at a time without distractions.

The role that I was about to take on was important not just for me but for the entire company. I was now starting to look at the bigger picture. I took all the boxes piled high old on my cushy leather chair and placed them on the floor without breaking my back. The boxes were very heavy and somewhat bulky. They appeared to be bursting at the seams. As I picked up the last box on the chair to place it on the floor, it split and crumbled in my bare hands, and papers were flying all over the place. The papers were jumping out of their folders and landing in every conceivable inaccessible location. I gave up and planked myself on my leather chair in total exhaustion. I just needed to rest for a minute.

    I began looking around in my office, and I noticed it was the same size office as the one I left before I went on my interview. Funny thing about that is that my office remained the same size, but my job description changed. I didn't move in to Lynn's office, which was almost twice the size of mine, and as I looked over, I see that office was empty. Why didn't they move me into that office with my promotion? I got up out of my office and looked at what appeared to be a nameplate on the door of Lynn's old office; the nameplate read "Coaching Room." Now I am really insulted. I didn't get the bigger office but only the bigger title. In fact, I didn't even talk to Russell about a pay increase. I was so excited about getting this job that I forgot to ask him about the money. I can settle that later. Right now, I have to go back in my office. I have to pick up all the paper that flew out of last box that I picked up and put them back in their proper folders.

    I started picking up the papers, one by one, and matching them up to all the folders that fell out of the last box I placed on the floor. I picked up a folder marked "Mike Feeney," where the papers had not fallen out of the folder as the folder was wrapped with Scotch tape and marked "Personal." At least that's what I thought it said until I took another quick look and the folder was marked "Personnel." For the life of me, I could not figure out why Lynn would have this folder in her office. What could she possibly have to do with Mike Feeney? In fact, she was Mike Feeney's replacement. I knew that Lynn knew she was a replacement for Mike Feeney. However, did Lynn know anything about the deal Russell made with Jonathan to send her, only for a short time as a loner until I was groomed for the job? Furthermore, did Mike know that Biotech had no intention of keeping Lynn but every intention to groom me for his job? Would he have ever left the position? And if he did, would he take legal action against Biotech for deceiving him and declaring him incompetent at his job after working in his position for over two decades?

    I needed to open the folder and see what was inside, and I needed to do it now. I needed answers, and I needed them now. That anxious feeling was coming over me once again. I did not know what to do. My emotions told me to take the tape off the folder. They told me to rip the elastic around the body of the folder and view the contents within. My hands began to tremble, and I began to perspire. I felt that rush of adrenaline going through me once again. Then, just like always, this calmness came over me where I took control of my emotions and my bodily functions. I became calm and poised and gently put the folder on my desk. Just as I did that, Russell walked into my office smiled at me as he pointed to the folder on my desk marked "Mike Feeney," and said, "I'll take that." Russell took the folder in his left hand as I handed it to him and, with his right hand, shook my hand and stated, "You just passed the first test. Congratulations!"

I did not have a clue of what Russell was talking about. What does he mean, "You just past the first test"? I did not how I was being tested by unpacking boxes and finding a folder containing Feeney's personal or personnel file whatever. This all seemed so bizarre. I really didn't like playing games about my life or my career. I was just like everyone else out there trying to get ahead and make a living. Now I am curious. What was in Feeney's file that Russell did not want me to see? Further, if the file was so secret, what was it doing in Lynn's stuff? I don't even know if these two people knew each other. The only thing I could think about was that Russell told Jonathan about Feeney and then had to tell Lynn why she was being loaned to Biotech. However, based on my discussion with Russell, Lynn only knew that she was going to replace Feeney, until a replacement was found for him. I wasn't aware that she would know that if Feeney did leave immediately, he would resign, and it wouldn't be obvious that he was terminated since it was so sudden. He could always say it was because of his heart problem that he had to leave suddenly. However, no one would believe him because of his giant ego.

I didn't know how much Jonathan shared with Lynn about me since she only worked with me for a few months. Did she realize that she was the guinea pig here? Did she know that Feeney would have fired me if Russell didn't step in and then deter my termination? All of these questions needed to be answered. I will not be able to rest until I know the truth behind this giant fiasco at Biotech. I am the victim here. Somehow, I felt I was on trial, on trial for what I didn't know, and I needed to find out soon. How do I approach Russell on this? What do I say to him? I am now in Lynn's old position, which is Mike Feeney's old position, and clueless about how I *really* got here. I needed answers, and I needed them fast.

Russell walked by my office about one o'clock and said to me, "Want to get a cup of coffee?"

I said, "Sure, when do you want to go?"

Russell looked at me, smiled, and said, "Now, five minutes from now or when you feel you are ready to go." Before I could answer, Russell already started walking toward the cafeteria, which was about fifty yards away from my office and mumbled softly, "It's all within your control." This statement really infuriated me, and I wanted to lunge for Russell as he was walking away from me. His statement kind of sent me back to when Jonathan asked me the same question back in the airport at LAX last Friday.

Why does everyone think that I need control at all times to be effective? I didn't see that in myself. All I asked Russell was when he wanted to go for the coffee. This was not inferred that in any way shape or form. *Am I a control freak?* I just asked a simple question that required a simple answer. I caught myself chopping my words to myself as I was saying them one at a time. This was ridiculous. I was getting too self-conscious about everything I said, and it didn't mean I needed to be in control. Enough already! I logged off my computer and now start heading toward the cafeteria. I looked for Russell, and he was nowhere to be found. I was furious. I didn't believe he stood me up. He specifically asked me to meet him for coffee in the cafeteria, and here I was.

He did say he would meet me here. I felt like he's trying to make a fool out of me. I had a whole office full of my junk and Lynn's junk to unpack and sort out. I didn't have time to play games. However, Russell is the COO, and I needed to wait for orders under duress, I might add.

Finally, I see Russell in the distance talking to the receptionist, who sat about fifty yards from the cafeteria. Therefore, you might say that my office is one hundred yards from the receptionist station equidistant from the cafeteria fifty yards in the other direction. So why am I telling you all this? I am telling you all this because Lynn Marconi and Russell Hampton just walked by me in the cafeteria heading toward my office without even checking to see if I was in the cafeteria. Russell must've told her that I was waiting for him in the cafeteria! Also, what is she doing here? I thought she was supposed to be back in California at Medical Solutions. I am not only angered; I am really confused. Both of these turkeys just walked by me, didn't even acknowledge that I existed, and now sitting, waiting for me in my own office.

I am so angry that anxious feeling is returning to me. I wanted to go back in my office and just tell them that I quit. This wasn't a game anymore, and I didn't find it very humorous. I needed to know what's going on, and I needed to know now! I needed to calm down before I walked in there. I didn't want to go into my office like a raving lunatic. I needed to be poised. I needed to be structured. Mostly, I needed to go in there as a professional leader in this organization. I needed to put my emotions aside right now and only focus on the facts. I walked into this place this morning thinking that I was going to get fired.

I found that I was part of a bigger picture and that my perception of things was much different than the reality of them. Okay, here it goes. I am now walking toward my old office.

My first impulse is to rush back into my office as I was standing in the middle of the cafeteria. From the distance, I see Russell and Lynn sitting in my old office or, should I say, my present office. The office that was no bigger than the one I would be leaving after I got fired. Or the same one I occupied after I received word I was getting a temporary promotion with a promise of permanency in a new position that was the result of a promotion. Either way, the office size, texture, and substance were unchanging. The only things that were changing were the chemicals that were processing information that was going through my brain right now at a mile a second.

I needed to sit down for a minute before I charged to my office with Russell and Lynn waiting for me. After all, they never announced that they were going in my office and virtually walked right by me two minutes ago. Further, Russell never told me that Lynn was coming in to Biotech today. This is all happening way too fast, and I really needed to sort things out. That adrenaline was starting to run through me one more time. I was getting anxious, and the palms of my hands were beginning to sweat. I felt kind of lightheaded, and my heart was racing in my chest. Suddenly, everything in the cafeteria is spinning around, and I felt like I was going to pass out. I was powerless to move and somehow managed to find the chair in the cafeteria before I fell on the floor. *What is happening to me?* I was losing control of myself, and I needed to get it back. My body wasn't doing what my mind was telling it to do! I was a physical and mental wreck, and my former and future bosses were sitting in my past, present, and perhaps future office! As I began to relax a little bit when finally the anxiety attack subsided, I happened to see something very interesting outside the cafeteria window where I was sitting. I looked up at a giant oak tree, not far from the cafeteria window diagonally across from our building. I noticed that on one of the branches of the tree, there was a robin's nest. I observed the mother robin feeding a worm to one of her offspring. I also observed her (after several prompts and pushes) fly away from the nest and let another of her offspring fly away on its own.

In this instance, a picture was worth a thousand words. It really made me think about the meaning of leadership and made me wonder whether or not there was a leadership gene. What did Jonathan see in me that I didn't see? What did Russell see in me that I didn't see? What did Lynn observe in me that I didn't see in me? Most importantly, why is it that I didn't see what they saw and observed in me?

All of these thoughts were running through my head as my body began to regain its composure. Interestingly enough, I didn't have to tell my body to regain its composure. It just kind of did it on its own. The mother robin in the nest didn't read the instruction book on how to be told that she needed to feed one of her offspring and send the other one off to find its way in the world. There were no intense training sessions with large classes and three-hundred-page manuals with twenty-five guest speakers to dictate how and why things should be done.

I was now beginning to realize in an extremely short period the differences between management and leadership. Before manuals were written and rules and regulations were created, an individual or group of individuals figured out what works for them in a corporation to be successful and profitable. These individuals all had the leadership gene, and they knew what worked for them. They also had a certain learning style and were only successful based on their abilities and no one else's. Essentially, what these individuals did was keep recorded documents on what made them successful in the forms of training manuals and intuitive steps that provided for their success. Therefore, their predecessors would assume that what they wrote down and recorded would make others successful as well.

It is the job of the manager to essentially take these recorded steps and procedures and implement them by tasking their subordinates to carry them out in the same manner as their predecessors that first implemented them. If the manager does not receive the same results as his or her predecessor had intended when they wrote down what made them successful, the subordinates were charged with the inability to carry out the job tasks or functions. These subordinates are ultimately deemed to be incompetent or inefficient at their jobs.

The leader looks at things a little bit differently. Essentially, when you think about it, individuals are hired not only what we perceive they are capable of doing at present but, more importantly, what they can do for us in the future. Essentially, a good leader can instinctively pinpoint an individual's talents to be utilized down the road more than job skills. A leader digs deeper than the present need to be fulfilled when a new individual comes on board. A leader looks at a new hire more as a return on investment, rather than an expense on the balance sheet. All of this is going through my head right now, as if Dr. Phil was sitting across from me. I began to chuckle and laugh at myself and realize that I didn't have to be in control to have control. This all just happened naturally. I had no idea what Lynn and Russell were doing in my office, nor should I need or want to find out. I couldn't control this. I didn't choose for them to go to my office; they did. Therefore, I could just sit here for the next half hour and not worry about it. After all, I was on my coffee break.

As I continued to look out the window, I was thinking of something else. Everyone had a different learning style and a different learning curve. For example, no one told me that I was turning into a control freak. They told me that I like to have control. They didn't necessarily tell me this as a good or bad thing. It was just a trait that I have. I am beginning to realize that how I utilize this trait would dictate the difference between being a successful leader or a dominant manager. I was one to always believe that being labeled was a bad thing. It is important for me at this point to understand that I should not take any comments as negative until I am able to thoroughly research why and how the comments were made.

It is all beginning to come together now just because you have a three-hundred-page manual that made someone else successful, you should not assume that you will have the same successes as them based on your individual learning curve. If your learning curve is not the same as your predecessors that designed a product or service that was proven to be successful, then you don't give up on your goals and aspirations. You then need to be innovative and creative and discover what it is that works for you. When you are creative and uninhibited, you think more clearly about yourself and what you are doing. You get a sense of challenge and exploration into uncharted waters that only you can manage and change.

I need to somehow realize my learning curve. If others believe in me, why am I finding it so hard to believe in me? I guess I found the answer to my control problem. I need to reaffirm who I am first before I decide what to do next in my career. I am okay with that.

LEADERSHIP LESSONS

Josh is going through quite a range of emotions in this chapter. Just as he begins to understand the nature of leadership, his ego gives rise to his old insecurities. A leader gains fulfillment from the accomplishments of his team, not from larger offices, higher compensation, and executive perks. These external rewards come with success but are not the primary driver for a leader.

The term "leadership gene" appears for the first time here, raising the question whether leaders are born or made. In the opinion of the author, the answer is a resounding yes. Many of us come into the workplace with the intelligence, knowledge, and empathy necessary for leadership. To turn these attributes into leadership requires constant practice and observation of those we have chosen as role models.

No learning path is ever smooth; we will all revert to our earlier behaviors at times. No learning path is ever complete. Each of us continues to improve our leadership skills throughout our careers.

Chapter 8

FINDING THE LEADERSHIP GENE

Someone once said, "To thyself be true." I haven't established the real Josh Keating as yet. I am sitting here in the cafeteria, looking out a window when my past and present bosses are in my office and I am not in that office with them. The question is *why*. Simply, all I needed to do was walk about one yard out of this cafeteria to my destination and greet Lynn and Russell. The only thing that was preventing me from doing that right now was me. No one was restraining me or preventing me from walking to my office. I was free to do whatever I wanted within the confines of my own mind. Yes, I made that choice, and I didn't need to be prompted in order to do so. So the question is, why am I a physical and emotional wreck when there is no need to be? What is truly the crisis that is preventing me from getting answers to mysteries I cannot solve? You know, I really can't come up with an answer.

I got up from my chair in the cafeteria, and I started to walk toward my office. I no longer felt inhibited and anxious as I did when I walked to the cafeteria to meet Russell earlier today. There was no rush of adrenaline, and I really felt focused. Interestingly enough, I now feel a sense of control but in a very different way. The control I felt before my visit to the cafeteria focused on what was going on around me and feeling helpless and alienated when I didn't know or understand events I experienced, when I had no prior knowledge of them. For example, I didn't know why I felt deceived or alienated from knowing that Russell had invited Lynn to Biotech without telling me. First of all, I have to realize that Russell was not obligated to tell me anything that has to do with his personal agenda. He may tell me out of courtesy, but that's all. Therefore, my controlling habits precipitated an emotional reaction to Lynn's visit rather than an observation that a meeting was going to take place with Russell.

I was now realizing that I was not getting the answers to what I need to learn about being an effective leader at Biotech. The answers were not coming easy. However, I was discovering more and more about myself and the role I played in this company. I was now realizing that so many people were investing in me because they believed in me. They wanted me to be in control of myself but for different reasons. They wanted me to lead others, not by controlling them but by helping them discover who they were more importantly than the role they played in the organization. Their roles in the organization would become much more meaningful and much more effective because I showed them what they needed to do by example rather than tell them. Therefore, they can become more innovative and more creative in the process of learning how to be leaders themselves. They can discover their own leadership gene as I was discovering right now. Then they could transfer their leadership skills to their successors as the legacy of the leadership gene continued. I was realizing that this is what leading is all about. It's not about telling. It's about doing. It's not about reacting but about acting at the proper time at the proper place, without being prompted. It's about giving direction rather than looking for it. Most importantly, you don't have to dig for the gene. It's in your own backyard.

I am thinking all this in the time it took me to walk the hundred yards from the cafeteria to my office. I finally arrived at my office, refreshed and uninhibited. To my surprise, Lynn and Russell had migrated over to the conference room behind closed doors. I felt the adrenaline beginning to flow inside me once again. Believe me, this was an unsolicited reaction in me that I could not control. However, I was always one to believe that is the mind that controls the body and not the other way around. Once again, I found myself in a holding pattern as my target audience was no longer in my office.

One of the important things that I learned about leadership is—unplanned events are customary for successful leaders to handle. The question here is whether or not I was waiting for an event to occur if Lynn and Russell had remained in my office. I think I was putting too much of the focus on myself and not on their purpose for being here. It's not all about me, is it?

If I took the focus off myself, I may begin to look at the bigger picture. Purpose was not defined by individuals. Rather, purpose was defined through innovation and creative thought. Purpose start with "vision" before it is defined by "mission."

My task right now was to continue unpacking all these boxes and sorting my files and Lynn's files. *I am dying to know what is going on with Lynn and Russell right now!* I can't help but think, *Why is Lynn here?* Again, that feeling of adrenaline was flowing in my body, and to make matters worse, I saw someone. Who do I see walking by my office heading toward the conference room? Walking by my office right now was the my worst nightmare with no rhyme or reason. In amazement, I was watching no other than Mike Feeney walking by my office. I can't believe what my eyes were observing right now. However, in this case, perception was reality. Mike looked rather pale and gaunt. He also appeared very thin from my observation. Although I had not seen him in a few months, I know something was wrong with him. I observed Mike taking a seat outside of the conference room as I continued to unpack boxes. I didn't know if he even saw me in my office. *I am sure he would've said hello or something. Here I go again censoring everybody's actions and reactions around me. Now, I am conscious of doing this every time I turn around. I am sure it has something to do with that control thing.*

I continued to unpack boxes, and every set of documents that I unpacked blended into the next set. I was too focused on why Feeney's here today and more focused on why Lynn was here today. *I know this can't be all about me, right?* Here I go again thinking about me. *What difference does it make who this is about? I have a job to do!* I now began to get a little curious as to why Feeney was here as that calmness returned to me. I was no longer feeling anxious; it must be the chemical imbalance in my brain. I continued to unpack boxes, and I noticed that Feeney was no longer sitting outside on the conference room. However, the door to the conference room remained shut. Suddenly my cell phone rang playing the ring tone for *Gilligan's Island*. I picked up my phone and answered, "Hello?" I heard Russell's voice on the other end of the phone while conversation was ensuing in the background.

Russell stated, "Josh, are you busy?" I responded nonchalantly that I was still unpacking boxes. Russell stated, "Josh, drop what you're doing, and please come into the conference room."

I immediately charged toward the conference room and briskly knocked on the door. I see the shadow of Lynn coming to the door and opening it abruptly. She was smiling in a very professional manner as she did when she was greeting clients when I was working for her. She said, "It's great to see you, Josh, you look wonderful!" Before I could say anything, she went back to her seat and abruptly crossed her legs as she sat down, staring at some documents on the conference room table. Mike Feeney sat there motionless, staring at me in a kind but pensive manner. As I looked closer at him, I noticed that he had big circles around his eyes looking as if he hadn't slept for months. I returned the smile rather nervously and just looked at my folded hands on top of the conference room table. Russell cleared his throat and nervously scratched his neck as if to treat an irritated neck from a heavily starched shirt collar. He took off his glasses and just observed everyone sitting around that conference table. He didn't say a word. He just observed. He cleared his throat one more time and took a sip of water from a glass filled with ice cubes floating around a wedge of freshly sliced lemon. He then stated in a very low and melancholy manner, "Josh, I suppose you're wondering why I asked Lynn and Mike to meet me here today." As I shrugged my shoulders and looked Russell straight in the eye, I was definitely at a loss for words. In fact, even if I wanted to speak, I didn't think anything would come out of my mouth. How was it possible for me to give an answer when I didn't even understand the question? At this point, I felt like I was in the twilight zone and have lost touch with reality. What I was seeing and hearing made no sense to me at all. When I first came here this morning, my intent was to see whether or not I still had a job. I found that in a few short hours, I was fired, rehired, promoted, and now sitting in the conference room with two of my former bosses and my future boss (if that is possible). I felt like this was some sort of game where I had to prove myself in order just to stay in touch with reality.

Russell looked directly at me in a very pensive manner and said to me, "Josh, I asked Lynn to come here today to explain to her that Jonathan and I have been friends for many years—she was asked to come here to help sort things out while Mike Feeney recuperated from complications stemming from a long-standing heart condition. Mike now has a clean bill of health but cannot return to work in the same modality and position that he previously had prior to leaving Biotech several months ago."

I looked back up at Russell after staring at my folded hands on the conference throughout his explanation about Mike and said to him, "Russell, I really feel like I have been duped. I don't know what to say and what to make out of all of this! I feel very much like a pawn on a chessboard." I now felt the adrenaline really starting to flow, and I didn't know how to control it.

Russell looked at me very pensively and said, "Take it easy, Josh. No one is trying to dupe you. Take a look around you. You notice that two individuals sitting with us in this room have gone out of their way to be here to meet with you today." I was ready to open my mouth and say something else, when Russell continued and said, "Do you really think that your main goal coming into work today was to sit in an office you occupied before you decided to go on an interview to work for another company?" I looked at Russell, and I could feel my feet and my hands beginning to shake, and my whole body felt like jelly. Russell went on to say, "Do you realize that in any other company, they would've looked at the series of events going on that justified us letting you go because of your lack of motivation at the job for six months or more prior to when you went on that interview on the West Coast?" I just sat there with my mouth open, looking at Russell in total amazement and embarrassment. He went on to say, "Why do you think we kept you here and you are sitting in the conference room at Biotech right now?"

At this point, I wanted to crawl on my belly out of that room and jump into some ocean and submerge myself for eternity. I could feel the adrenaline getting more intense and anxiety beginning to spin my head once again. I could see everything in the wrong starting to close in on me and the beads of perspiration I could feel falling down from my face and around the shirt collar of my neck. I was powerless to move, and I just did it to oblivion. Looking at the wall with my hands folded on top of the conference room table, I was motionless and speechless when Mike looked at me in total compassion and kindness. He no longer had that mean look on his face. He was poised and relaxed and poured some ice water into his glass and sat back in his chair in a very relaxed manner.

He paused for a moment, looked around the room, and gently looked up at me and said, "Josh, I owe you an apology. And I wanted to do it today, knowing that you were returning to the office after being notified by Lynn that you will be starting back to work today." I could feel myself choking up as my feelings of retaliation and resentment flushed out of my body like a bad fever. I felt myself starting to relax again and that calmness return to my body as it had done several times over the past seventy-two to ninety-six hours.

Mike went on to say, "Josh, for over four years that you have worked for me, I never realized who you were because I didn't know who I was. I always had to be in control of others because I couldn't control myself. I never trusted anyone and believed that no one trusted me. I micromanaged everything I did. I felt that if I made a mistake, it would reflect on everyone, including me. You see, I wanted to be perfect." I looked at Mike in total amazement, not believing this could be coming from him. I was ready to say something when he put his hand up and said, "Please let me finish. I was only looking at the negatives and realized that I never gave you any positive feedback. I wanted you to be like me and protect you so that you wouldn't fail." I looked at him and asked him why he never said anything to me about that. I asked him if he felt that I was unapproachable and that he couldn't talk to me. Mike told me—he was afraid to talk to me because he felt it would make him appear to me as though he didn't have control and that he was a poor leader.

I could feel the adrenaline beginning to flow in my body again. I needed to find out why Mike felt this way about me and why I threatened him so much. I just didn't know if this was the time and place to bring that out. Considering how he looked and his present state of mind, it might not be a good idea. At that point, Russell stepped in and began to speak. Mike put his hand up and said, "Russ, please let me finish." Russell gestured with an open hand back to Mike as if to politely tell him he could continue. Mike went on to say that he has had an ongoing cardiac problem for over a year and a half, and the timing was perfect for him to let me go because I was causing him so much stress because we could not agree on anything. Mike explained that just before Lynn came in to work for Biotech, he had a meeting with Russell and explained all the reasons why I should be terminated from my job. Michael explained that he had given

Russell several write-ups about my performance and had detailed documentation of why I should be terminated. He told me that he really thought he had a solid case to terminate me.

    I just stared at Mike in total amazement when he was telling me all of this. The adrenaline was flowing so bad in my body that I wanted to strangle the living daylights out of Mike. I couldn't believe what my ears were hearing. I just sat there continuing to listen. The adrenaline was out of control, and I just wanted to get up strangle the living daylights out of Mike despite his medical condition. However, something was holding me back. I can't explain it, but something just didn't sit right with me. I got the strange feeling that Mike wasn't telling me everything. There was no rationale, rhyme, or reason for my feeling. I just felt uneasy and surprisingly less anxious.

    My instincts told me that there was something else going on besides the words that were coming out of Mike's mouth right now. Why would he be hiding anything from me? Why am I feeling this way? It just doesn't make sense. However, surprisingly, I am feeling that calmness come over me, despite all the things that Mike was telling me. Apparently, I was less focused on my feelings and more on what Mike had to say regarding his behavior toward me. This is a paradoxical shift on how I usually react when this type of verbiage is directed at me. I would always take criticism rather harshly and personally. However, my bitterness suddenly disappeared, as did my anger. I felt more poised and confident right now, more than I have been in a long time, and this does not make any sense to me. I continued to listen to Mike and tried to rationalize why he would be telling me all of this in front of the CEO and the person who temporarily took his place and suddenly left the company, after two months of employment. My attention was more focused on why a guy who was been on my case so many years and admitting now that he was trying to fire me has such a sudden change of heart. My curiosity had now peaked, but in a different way. When something was out of the ordinary, despite how uncomfortable it might be such as constant criticism and negative feedback, you look for deviations from the norm rather than the norm.

I realized that by being less focused on myself, I was beginning to assimilate facts and make more productive observations around my environment. Russell now intervened into the conversation at the conference table, while Lynn continued to remain extremely quiet throughout all of this. Every once in a while she would look up and smile when she was not writing. However, she never really said much throughout the entire meeting. Somehow, instinctively, I looked over at Lynn and said, "Did you know any of this about Mike?"

Russell immediately interjected and said while looking at me with the cold blank stare, "That question is totally out of place at this meeting, Josh!"

I looked over at Russell and said, "With all due respect, sir, I don't think the question is inappropriate at all!" Before Russell could say anything, Lynn looked at me directly after briefly glimpsing over at Russell and said to me in a very poised manner, "I am not at liberty to discuss that right now, Josh. I think that a question of this nature should be addressed on another venue and at another time." Lynn looked back down at her notepad and continued writing and taking notes.

    Although I was not comfortable with Lynn's answer. I did instinctively plant a seed in both Lynn and Russell, which made them come out of their comfort zones and react to my question in an unexpected manner. I began to sense a feeling of intense uneasiness in the conference room from Lynn and Russell. Yet I sensed a feeling of intense sadness and disappointment from Mike Feeney, which made no sense at all to me since he told me everything I needed to know. Although it was very painful and uncomfortable for me to hear, it seemed sincere and honest. I was thankful for that. Russell stated unless there was anything else, the meeting was ended for that day, but we would resume two more times, and he gave us calendar dates that spread over the next four weeks. Lynn had to adjust for traveling and start packing. Russell thanked me in the conference room as everyone else left the room with him.

    Only Lynn and I remained in the room, and she continued packing her things. The conference door was still open. As I walked toward the open door to exit the room, I instinctively looked back at Lynn, who was my boss for the past few months before all this happened. I remembered my last encounter with her at LAX where I was to meet a client she was going to visit when suddenly she had to return back to Boston. Lynn looked up at me and smiled, and our eyes locked for a fleeting second. Suddenly and nervously, Lynn looked at me in a trembling voice, which was totally out of character for her and blurted out, "What, Josh!"

I blurted back at her, "What about what?" I said.

She snapped back at me, "Why did you look at me when you left the room?"

I blurted back, "Why, what is so unusual about that?"

She smiled nervously and replied, "Nothing, I guess."

I then started walking back toward her in the room, and as I was walking, I said to her, "Are you okay, Lynn?"

She said, "Yes, no, I guess…" She said this all in the same breath, which made no sense at all to me.

I then said instinctively, "What is it that you're not telling me, Lynn?"

Lynn blurted back at me, "Nothing, absolutely nothing, and stop badgering me." Lynn's eyes began to fill, and I saw a tear coming down her cheek as she nervously continued to pack her belongings and notepad into her briefcase and her travel pack. I began walking away from her, and I could feel the emotion rising in me as well as if we were sharing the same feelings. However, I had no clue of what she was thinking, but somehow, I felt what she was feeling. I realized, for the first time in my life, I made the *human connection*. I also discovered my leadership gene.

My reaction to Lynn just now made me realize a whole bunch of things about myself. The first thing made me realize is that I was human and not just concerned about the situation at hand but also for the individuals the situation was affecting. I also realize that I should not remain in my own silos and look at how all situations affect me but rather how I affect all other situations by decisions that I make. I also learned that everything was not about how I perceive the facts but rather how the facts open doors to giving answers to the truth. In retrospect, the most valuable lesson that I learned here is that although I haven't pieced all of the facts together as yet, I feel confident that understanding the human element will bring out the truth in all the mysterious happenings that occurred in the past few weeks from the time I decided to interview for a different job.

LEADERSHIP LESSONS

As we've discussed, trust is the most important element in leadership. It is essential that both the leader and the led work hard to establish mutual trust. Here we see Josh observing conversations that may (or may not) be about him; he assumes that he is the subject of the discussion and that the comments are negative. One can argue whether the assumption is because the leaders haven't given Josh reason to trust them or because Josh is not able to bring himself to trust. The answer to this question is irrelevant; without trust, the relationship will inevitably fail.

A leader must clearly demonstrate that his purpose in providing feedback is to help the employee reach his personal goals rather than to criticize his faults. Russell does not accomplish this with comments like "You passed your first test" or by acting mysteriously. The employee must realize that he is not always the subject of every discussion and action. Josh's belief that Russell and Lynn were talking about him was not supported by any evidence. Surely they have other business issues that have to be decided. Even if Russell were an ideal leader, Josh would not be receptive to trust in these circumstances.

Chapter 9

THE DICHOTOMY OF PERCEPTION

Now that I have discovered all this about myself, what do I do with this newfound leadership gene? I discovered that the gene is assimilation through the human connection. Let me explain what I mean by this because it is complicated unless you experience it yourself.

From the time I began telling you my story, you know that I was hard pressed to communicate with people on a level that I felt comfortable communicating, despite where I was or what I was doing. I was always tense and never at ease because I plainly just was not comfortable being around people I didn't know, even people that I did know. I was always wondering what they would be thinking about me. I always felt that I was being judged. Therefore, my nature was to always be skeptical about anyone within a six-block radius of my inner circle. I lived in mental seclusion and a world of don't trust anyone and always be on your guard. My purpose for existence was based on my core values that I have learned and have agreed to abide by for the rest of my life. This was my comfort zone and up until now, had no reason to come out of it.

Boy, what a day this was! The meeting in the conference room really got to me. Here I was sitting with my former bosses, the CEO of my company, and really had no a clue why I was invited into the meeting today. I know this sounds lame, but I still think there was something missing from today's conversation that I was supposed to hear for some reason. Who really wanted me at that meeting today and why? Why was Lynn flown in today to meet with Russell? What is the "big picture" plan here? If Mike is so sick, why would he be looking to come back to work but not in the position he once had? This really raises my eyebrows, at least for the time being. In the past, I would've never asked these types of questions. I always would go with the flow. As long as I was getting a paycheck, I was okay. So with a great boss like Lynn and Mike being out of my life forever, why am I here asking all these questions and upsetting the applecart when I have the opportunity to step into my former bosses' (both of them) position? What is in it for me? Why do I need to probe further?

I look around me and take a look at the empty conference room that Lynn just left. Over the years, I have been in this conference room thousands of times with Mike, getting reprimanded and belittled for crazy, stupid things. So why am I so concerned now about stupid stuff that really doesn't concern me? Why can't they let me just do my job and be on with it? I have more than paid my dues and ready to step up into my new position with the guidance of my coaches, Mike and Lynn.

Two weeks have gone by since our meeting, and I have yet to get Lynn out of my mind. Her reaction to my questions, just before she left to go back to LAX, made me very uncomfortable. It was not like her to ride the emotional wagon. She was always poised and had control over any given situation. However, that wasn't the case two weeks ago in the conference room with Russell, Mike, and myself. This is what happens when you discover your leadership gene. I told you earlier, my leadership gene was assimilation through the human connection. I believe the gene was now beginning to make me look at things differently. My perceptions were beginning to change on how I looked at people and the world in general. No, I wasn't born again. No, I wasn't taught how to find a leadership gene. I found it because somebody planted a seed in me without realizing that he had. Somehow, someway, I couldn't help but think that Jonathan had something to do with that meeting we had with Mike Feeney in the conference room two weeks ago. There was nothing logical that helped me make that connection that was factually sitting in front of me. I just realized it right now because my reality did not match my perception. Rather, my perception will help me lead to my reality by taking me out of my silos and help me assimilate the bigger picture without me being in the center of it.

Let's see. I was born August 3, 1981, and in 1997, I was only sixteen years old. I remember a movie I saw based on a novel written by Carl Sagan entitled *Contact*. The movie starred Jodie Foster as a young scientist who lost her dad when she was nine years old and her mother died from complications of childbirth. Up until she was nine years old, Jodie Foster's role playing the character of Eleanor Arroway was to begin her journey understanding the cosmos and looking for extraterrestrial life with the assistance of her dad who supported her efforts. Tragically, in the movie, Eleanor's dad suffered myocardial infarction (heart attack) and died leaving Eleanor absolutely alone in her world and in the universe. In the movie, Eleanor grew up to become a brilliant young scientist, graduating magna cum laude from MIT with her doctorate and declining a tenured position at Harvard University to look for and research extraterrestrial life in the cosmos. She worked in a program that was called SETI (search for extraterrestrial intelligence).

Eleanor basically cut herself off from the rest of the world, and look at every decision that she made, every action that she took, and every idea that she formulated be calculated and planned. For example, when Eleanor's father passed away, she blamed herself because she did not have the medicine he needed in a medicine chest that was close enough so she could get to it sooner in order to save his life. She denounced the fact that it was God's will that her father died and was out of her control. Yes. Eleanor was a scientist and a very good one, with strong hope and determination. She had the resiliency to accomplish whatever needed to be done and prove to the world that there was life on other planets, on other galaxies, and she would be the one to find it. Her leadership gene was clearly resiliency, and you could also say that there was some hint of total accountability and that gene was hers to own. The gene never remained dormant. It was always manifested from the time she was a little girl with her dad. The interesting thing was that it was Eleanor's belief that the gene did not need to experience anything that was supported without scientific data. In her mind, there was a quantitative measure to every equation and a logical answer for every observation. Yet in her character role in the movie, she was seeking to find extraterrestrial life when the scientist who initially funded and supported her program SETI decided to pull the plug on the project because there was nothing substantial to support her data and continue funding the program that she worked in.

Once the plug was pulled on the program, she had nowhere to go and tried endlessly and feverishly to secure funding. However, she refused to give up even if she had to search for extraterrestrial life alone; she would not stop even if he killed her. Many of the parts of the movie were vague in my mind because I saw this so long ago. However, as Eleanor was making her last ditched effort and practically begs for funding in a company called Hadden Industries, she was once again turned down for support in her project. The financial board of this company did not seem to believe that it was worth the investment to fund her research. She made an emotional and driving plea to the committee, asking them to have just a tiny bit of vision, insight into changing a world where we might be able to share other planets and know who we are and what are our purposes in our roles at work, in our lives, and our existence. She goes on to talk about how crazy things such as flying machines, televisions, radios, etcetera came from ideas that didn't really have a solid mathematical foundation to prove that they would work. However, their founders had vision to look into the future and know that they could make changes that would not just better themselves but those that surrounded them. Yes, the perceptions of these authors did not meet the realities of their audience when they made their presentations. However, in the movie *Contact*, Eleanor Arroway's presentation was heard by no other than Mr. Hadden, the entrepreneur, owner, and visionary of Hadden Industries. Mr. Hadden had agreed to fund Eleanor's project.

Eleanor subsequently was sent to a planet called Vega, whose inhabitants took the form of her dad to explain to her that she was not alone in the universe, and all we have is each other in the loneliness of space.

Wow! I really don't know why I just thought of all of that, but I do remember that the movie ended when the control station who launched the rocket that sent Eleanor to this planet Vega said that the rocket had malfunctioned, and she never really went into space. She made a plea to the world to believe her that she had experienced this wonderful journey that proved that we were not alone in the universe. Yes, no one believed her. The cards were reversed. She now was the one that had the vision. She now was the one who made the connection. Yet no one believed her. As a scientist, she had to agree with her constituents that what she was saying had no substantial quantitative proof that she even left the launch site, but yet she experienced something that was very wonderful. It was a connection that she never thought she had; it was something that was so beautiful that she couldn't even describe it, but yet she could share it.

My perception in my reality is now coming into focus. I am experiencing something wonderful. I am experiencing my leadership gene. It needs to be nurtured. It needs to be coached. It needs to be understood. It needs to be respected. It needs to be me. I realized that I have to start with me and understand my vision before I can get others to realize their visions. Visions may not be realities right now, but they will turn into realities later on. When those visions become realities, others will follow. We call this successorship.

My leadership gene of assimilation refers to assimilation of facts, and I do this through the people connection. There is no other way to exercise the intuitive in conjunction with the facts as they are presented. There is absolutely no rationale or congruency as to why I think that Jonathan had something to do with Mike Feeney being in the conference room two weeks ago with the CEO. There is absolutely no connection but making it in my mind. I do know that Russell and Jonathan took similar paths before they went on to become leaders in their companies. I do know that Mike Feeney reported to Russell. I do know that I reported to Mike. I do know that after Mike got sick that I reported to Lynn. I do know that although Lynn treated me quite nice that I needed a change from the company I was working in and went to a company for an interview where I had absolutely no idea that there was a connection with the company I am working for now. I could've gone to interview at any company but just happened to choose the one that Jonathan worked for. Is there such a thing as fate?

Something about the way that Lynn lost it when I asked her if she knew anything made me even more curious, especially now. As they say, I was lost in translation. I needed to know more, but first, I need to do some more reflective thinking about why I am in this equation and why the players who are in the conference room two weeks ago were telling me things that were kept dormant for years. I highly doubt if they were looking for their leadership genes, a few weeks ago. There is something rotten in Denmark as they say, and I need to get to the bottom of this. Really, Mike should've had me fired. Based on his state of mind, if Jonathan and Russell communicated with each other so well, they must share information together when people go to some social gatherings. Maybe I am getting paranoid, but I know there's a lot more to the story than it appears.

LEADERSHIP LESSONS

Josh is right—there is much more to every story than first appears. Here we see him struggling with the "why" issue. When we communicate with people on day-to-day operational level, it is often enough to know the facts of what happened. This is enough for a manager to instruct his employees on the steps needed to resolve the situation. However, if a leader is to communicate on a personal level, he needs to understand *why* those involved have acted as they did. This provides the basis for developing skills rather than simply changing behavior.

He is also beginning to realize what we mean by "vision." In the movie, Jodie Foster had a vivid vision of a universe with contact between worlds. Using a science-based factual approach, she was not able to win the support she needed. Lacking the organizational authority to force her plan on others, she failed. She finally succeeded by learning to communicate her vision on a personal level. People are not likely to follow a leader wholeheartedly unless they adopt the leader's vision on a personal level. A leader's goal is to help others grasp the vision and accept it as their own.

We are looking at some essential elements of the leadership gene. It requires having a vision of the future that you can communicate to those who will help make it happen. That requires a deep understanding of those on your team so that communication brings them to the same level of understanding that you have.

Chapter 10

MANAGERS DELEGATE THE FACTS AND LEADERS QUESTION THEM WHEN APPROPRIATE

I have almost completed unloading and categorizing all of the files in my same old office coupled with my new temporary promotion to director of operations (Lynn Marconi's old title). Before her, it was Mike Feeney, and here I am stuck in the middle between their two management styles. I also really don't know what I am doing in my new job, except that I could do my old one, a little bit better. By the way, since I could be my new boss and me, I actually find this to be a bit humorous as the only person I really report to is Russell and occasionally the assistance of Lynn. I am not really too sure what Mike Feeney is going to do when he comes back. But it will, however, be in some capacity that does not entail being my boss.

It is now 9:00 a.m., and as history has recorded, Mike Feeney in the old days would be looking at his wristwatch standing by my office door walking frantically into his office pretending to be busy, while he was really checking what time I reported to work. He never really said anything about tardiness or attendance when he was my boss. However, he would make it known to me that he knew how many minutes I might be late for work that day. Now that I look back on all of this, it really is kind of humorous since I don't punch a clock. It's that type of management style that literally would drive me crazy. It gave me the impression of working for a straw boss. A straw boss is basically a person that performs the duties of his or her job, plus supervises the actions of others, often without legitimate authority except that authority that is delegated from the manager of supervisor with legitimate authority. These are the people that pretty much are puppets and report back to the boss everything that is said or done in the department without the boss actually being there to witness it. These straw bosses are essentially taskmasters with no real leadership capabilities I find this to be a quite interesting dynamic at Biotech. However, I am sure that this type of management exist in many organizations. Some are larger and some smaller than this one.

Boy, it's nine o'clock in the morning, and I am sitting here with the latte pretty much on my own agenda. Well, I think I'll just continue unloading my "junk" and distribute them as I should, in my office. I remember a few weeks back when Russell took a packet from me marked "Mike Feeney." It was sort of a manila envelope with shoelace-like ties around it and never returned it to me. Why should I even really care what was it about that that I was so curious about. I really can't remember; all I remember is that he took it. Where he put it, I haven't the slightest clue. Why am I even thinking about this? I just have so much to unpack here, and I should not be fixated on any one thing. Okay, let's see now; it's now ten minutes after nine, and I feel like I have been in my office for three hours already. The question is, why am I still working for this company? I know because I am ambitious, smart and…what the heck was in that envelope I gave Russell that had Mike Feeney's name on it? I just can't get it off my mind.

I know that Russell will be in for a meeting at eleven o'clock with Mike Feeney, who is supposed to be coming back to work sometime this week. I'm not sure I even know what was wrong with him. In fact, I am wondering if he was even as sick as he said he was. Maybe he was just overstressed, had some marital problems, or something. I don't know I just feel very confused right now and I need to recoup my thoughts and stop focusing on how I feel. I can't be ruled by my emotions. I need time to put things in perspective and wonder why I am in this place at this time doing what I am doing stacking files on a shelf. Yes, I suppose this is why I got my MBA in finance. I got my MBA in finance so that I could be subservient to some really ridiculous plan that puts me in some type of superficial leadership and hangs me out to dry with no future. Why am I thinking like this? What is wrong with me? Let me say this out loud since there is nobody in my office right now. It'll make me feel better. "What is wrong with me?"

Suddenly, I turn, and I hear someone who is within breathing distance of me say, "I don't know. You tell me, Josh, what's wrong with you!" It was Jonathan. I didn't know whether to hug him are just scream out a sigh of relief to see him in the flesh when I needed him most. What a sight for sore eyes he was to see at this time. Jonathan looked at me and said, "Is everything okay, Josh?"

I looked back at him square in the eye and said, "Why, does it look like everything is not okay?"

He said, "I don't know. You tell me. You are the one that is asking, 'What is wrong with me?'"

I looked at Jonathan, and I chuckled and said to him in a very slow, methodical manner, "I am okay really, just venting a little."

Jonathan said, "Okay then, no foul, no harm." He turned away from me, walked out of my office toward the reception area, and greeted Russell as he came through the door. Following right behind Russell was Mike Feeney, whom I knew was meeting with Russell at eleven o'clock but had absolutely no idea that he was also meeting with Jonathan. Some strange connections had begun popping into my mind. Now I was thinking that there might have been more of a connection between Jonathan and Russell than I initially thought. Something now began to really bother me, and I didn't know why. I smelled a rat somewhere but didn't know where the rat was. I feel now like am writing a soap opera, and none of this is really making any sense to me. So why should I really care about the meeting that's going on with Mike, Russell, and Jonathan at eleven o'clock this morning.

What is interesting about this whole scenario is that I don't see Lynn anywhere. Why would I even think she should be included in this meeting? She was only working with me for a month as my temporary boss after Mike Feeney had left due to medical reasons. I can't get it out of my mind how she left our last meeting in such an emotional state, which was very out of character for her. People who are usually calm and collective do not come out of that calm and collective aura unless there's some very good reason to come out of it. Lynn was nowhere in sight, and somehow that made me very, very uncomfortable. Again, there is no substantial or quantitative reason why I should feel apprehensive about Lynn being absent from this meeting with Mike, Jonathan, and Russell. However, I was uncomfortable. I think what I will do is I will just go on and continue to put files on the shelf as I have been doing for the past hour and a half. I noticed that Mike was sitting outside of the conference room while Jonathan and Russell were having a closed-door discussion prior to their eleven o'clock meeting.

I signaled Mike to come into my office and sit down with me for a few minutes before his meeting. He smiled at me, and he had the same kind look he had when we left our meeting a couple of weeks ago. Once we put everything out on the table, he was fine with me. And it's like we were always best buddies. I can't believe I worked for him when he was such a tyrant for all those years and never knew how he really was on the inside. I never made that people connection with him. I never knew the type of person that he really was. I never had a chance to bond with him.

I asked Mike how things were going. He told me things were going very well, but he was recovering from his heart malady very slowly. He did however tell me that he was getting very bored and couldn't wait to come back, even on a limited basis. He told me that he would be assisting me on helping bridge the gap between his leadership and Lynn's and that he could do it rather quickly. Mike told me that he always thought that I was a quick study, and then I would go places with this company. I just looked up at him and chuckled. I couldn't help it. I said, "Mike, how can you say that when you always found the negative in what I did at work?" Mike looked at me and gave me a very long stare that broke into a sheepish smile.

He then chuckled and said, "If you only knew, Josh, how many times I wanted to tell you I felt that way about you and didn't." I couldn't believe what Mike was saying to me just now. Here he was telling me that he thought I would always go places in the company, but he never told me and always gave me negative feedback.

My next logical question was to ask him why he was always so negative. He thought I would go places and get promoted here. I didn't know why, but I suddenly locked up inside. I could not bring myself to ask Mike why he didn't speak up and why he didn't say anything to let me know how he really felt about me and my work. Perhaps my feelings of alienation toward him would have disappeared. If I really knew how he felt about me, things might have been different in our relationship over the past four years. Perhaps we would've gotten a lot more accomplished together if our relationship was more collegial than it was task orientated. In other words, Mike is the boss, he tells me what to do; I do it and answer to only please him and not what needs to be accomplished. I have to start getting all these terrible thoughts out of my head when Mike is opening up right in front of me just before his meeting.

There was a period of sustained silence when Mike and I just looked at each other. Finally, I chuckled back at Mike and also smiled but much less sheepishly. In fact, my smile was much more profound and exhilarating. I looked Mike square in the eye, and I said to him, "I am sorry that I failed you and let you know that I was hurting inside because I always thought you never thought I was worth the air that I was breathing." The smiles ran from both our faces into obscure contours of sadness and despair. I watched the color drain from Mike's face.

He looked up at me and said, "No, Josh, you don't get it! I failed you." I folded my hands on my desk and put my head down, staring at those folded hands.

I nodded my head back and forth and said softly and gently, "No, Mike, really, it's the other way around." I watched Mike sitting right in front of me, his eyes filling with tears and the cheeks of his face were reddened and his lips were trembling. I could see that around his collar, he was beginning to perspire. I thought he was going to have a heart attack, I swear.

I just looked at him, and I didn't move a muscle. I was so filled with emotion that I wanted to leap up over my desk and hug him until I could make the pain go away. This is a man that I have hated over the past four years for what he was doing to me. In reality, I realized that I was so focused on his behavior that I wasn't doing anything to change mine. This was a tragedy over the past several years and such a waste of time for the both of us. If we both picked up on the human connection where I found my leadership gene, things might have been a lot different between us. For the first time in my life, I realized that I could be human, and also be a leader. I also realized that you can't separate the two. In order to be an effective leader, you need to be human. I realize that we are human beings first and employees/employers second. All leaders need to realize this if they truly want to separate themselves from being straw bosses.

I looked up at Mike, and when I realized that he had settled down, I asked him if it would be okay if I stepped out for a minute to go to the restroom. He told me it was perfectly okay as he would be going into his meeting with Jonathan and Russell sometime in the next half hour. Mike asked me if it would be okay if he looked around my office while I was gone. I told him it was perfectly all right to look at anything he wanted to and that I had absolutely nothing to hide from him. I then chuckled, walked out of my office, and walked toward the restroom. I really didn't have to use the restroom. I just needed to get out of my office to think for a bit. The restroom was about five minutes from my office past the reception area. I just needed a few minutes to think through everything that just happened through my head.

For the first time in my life, I am realizing so many things about myself that I never knew. For example, I realized that the giant was more afraid of Goliath than the other way around. I also realized that I needed to let go of what I used to think was important and begin focusing on people more than planned events if I want to be a successful leader. I need to connect with people if I truly want to learn what people can do for themselves more than they could do for me or even the tasks they have been assigned. I am really starting to see the bigger picture now, and I like what I see. I feel good about myself and even about my encounter with Mike a few minutes ago.

I stopped by the cafeteria for a brief moment and grabbed myself a yogurt and a Chi tea for Mike, one sugar and two creams. I should know; I have been buying the same thing for him for the past four years. I regrouped myself and headed back to my office. When I entered my office, Mike was not sitting in the chair he was sitting in when I left to go to the restroom. My first impulse was to walk outside the office and look toward the reception area to see if I could see him. He was nowhere in sight. I looked at the conference room and didn't see him sitting at the conference room table. Where could he have gone? I thought I would sit in my office chair behind my desk and just wait for him. As I approached my chair, I stood looking stunned and at the floor in horror. Lying on the floor, turning blue with his hands clenched to his chest was Mike Feeney. Lying next to him on the floor was the manila envelope with the shoelace-type ties around it that Russell had asked me for when I was unpacking the files to put in my office not too long ago. The envelope was marked "Mike Feeney."

LEADERSHIP LESSONS

Too many managers still take their leadership lessons from the movie cliché tough drill sergeant. He takes great pains to establish his authority and motivates improvement by constantly pointing out weaknesses. Let's remember this is a character created by writers and actors who have never had to lead an organization.

Like most of us, Mike and Josh never questioned their tough guy and resentful subordinate roles. As a result, both have missed a great opportunity for personal development and professional success. Think of what Josh could have learned from Mike and what satisfaction Mike could have gotten from a close relationship with someone he respected. Think of the effect on Biotech and how much more effective the organization could have been.

Chapter 11

BRINGING THE LEADERSHIP GENE OUT OF DORMANCY

As I watched the life draining out of Mike Feeney's body, in the few seconds, I watched him die, time stood still. Nothing around me was real nor did it matter who or where I was. I was caught in a nexus where time and space didn't matter. The only two people that existed during this time freeze were Mike Feeney and me. I didn't feel guilt, shame, anger, remorse, fear, joy, pain, or anything connected with consequence or validation. I am not ashamed to say it, but I actually felt true and unconditional compassion for Mike. I knew in the pit of my soul that he would be gone very shortly. Yet his memory and his spirit would somehow live on in me and strengthen me for what was to come.

The next thing I remember hearing that snapped me out of everything was Jonathan yelling, "Call 911!" I remember Jonathan pounding Mike's chest and trying to administer CPR to him. However, it was too late. Mike had no pulse, and the paramedics took in a stretcher and confirmed his heart had stopped beating and asked the police to notify next of kin. Jonathan told me that just as I entered my office and before I sat down at my desk, he noticed a shoe sticking out in the distance from the conference room under my desk, and he thought I took my shoes off. He thought that I was in my office. However, when he saw me returning to my office with my shoes on, he knew it was not my shoe sticking out. He then walked to my office and saw me looking at the floor but motionless and in horror. He walked by me, he said, as I appeared to be in shock and immediately called 911. He then started to pound Mike's chest and breathe air into him. That's when I came out of shock I guess and waiting for the paramedics to pronounce Mike officially dead. You need to get a doctor to state you are clinically dead, meaning your brain has ceased to function.

Jonathan said they would wait for the medical report to determine the official cause of death from the coroner. He told me to relax as I was not suspect, at least not now, and heartily laughed out loud. I told him that he was not very funny and that I never saw anyone die before right before my eyes. The medical report finally came back. Mike had succumbed to a massive heart attack induced by an overdose of valium and alcohol. I was shocked. I never knew he even drank. He never had the smell of alcohol on his breath in the four years I worked for him. At least, I could not detect it. Anyway, Mike was gone. I had no clue as to why he had the manila envelope with the shoelace-type ties in his hand with his name on it when I found him on the floor. The next thing I know Russell joined us in my old office and said, "Lot of excitement for one day, ha?" I looked at him and didn't say anything. Funny, but my sense was that Russell didn't seem too disturbed about what just happened in the office. I thought it was quite traumatic.

Then, I thought, the envelope that Mike was holding in his hand with his name on it was not mentioned by either Russell or Jonathan when the incident occurred. I immediately asked Jonathan who was talking to Russell at the time and appeared to be somewhat distracted with my question about the envelope. You could even raise the issue of whether he was annoyed with me for asking. I asked, "Jonathan, did you see the envelope with Mike's name on it when the paramedics moved the body? I know you came in the office and saw me stunned over Mike's dying body." Jonathan looked at me as if I had three heads.

He said, "What envelope are you talking about?"

I looked at Jonathan stunned and said, "The envelope with Mike's name on it with the shoelaces wrapped around it."

Jonathan said, "Josh, go home and get some rest really. You are out of it." The contour of his face ran dry, and he took on almost another personality. His demeanor was methodical and purposeful, and he was focused on company business. It was like attacking an impenetrable fortress.

In a state of panic, I looked at Russell and said, "Did you see a manila envelope with Mike's name on it?" Russell looked at me and then looked at Josh without saying a word. I asked the question again. This time, I was looking directly into Russell's eyes without *flinching* a muscle. I was serious, and I was not going to move from the spot where I was standing until I got an answer. Russell excused himself from Mike and asked me to meet him in the conference room in ten minutes, and he would explain everything to me. He gave me a sheepishly kind smile that made me suspect he was going to let me in on the circle of all the peculiar things that has been going on since I returned from LAX on a job interview that everyone knew that was "not" going to happen except me and a guy I worked with and hated for over four years drop dead before my eyes. And to boot, hold an envelope in his hand with his name on it that disappeared after I saw him dying with it in his hand.

I needed some answers, and I didn't know why any of this was happening. I needed some guidance and some honest answers. Really, if I didn't get some honest answers soon and those in leadership positions become accountable to my questions, then I have no place here in this organization. I really believe that leaders should be as accountable to their subordinates as their subordinates to them. I really don't like being made a fool of. And I certainly do not take what just happened lightly. I really don't know why Russell was acting the way he was, and Jonathan reacted to me in a very bizarre manner, unlike the personality that I've known him since I met him at LAX.

I sat outside the conference room, waiting patiently for Russell to come in and explain everything to me as he stated. However, he never showed up. I went back into the area where the paramedics had taken Mike's body out of the building, and I was looking for both Mike and Jonathan. I could not find either one of them. I went to my office, and I waited patiently for another twenty minutes to half an hour. Still, no one showed up, and there was no Russell in the conference room to explain things to me. This whole fiasco was turning into something that I could've never thought up even in the most wildest of my dreams. I didn't understand any of this. However, I do believe one thing that I was taught at a very young age by my mother, who stated, "What goes around comes around."

I finally gave up waiting for Russell. I went back to my office, and I continued to load files, tons and tons of files. The last thing I remembered was how kind Mike Feeney was to me just before he died. I saw and observed the remnants of an amazing human being that I never really got to know. I wish I had more time to ask him more questions. And you know what? I wouldn't have wanted to ask him more questions about his job or what happened with the company. I know that eventually it will be found out what really happened with Mike Feeney. The types of questions I would've liked to have asked him would be related to how he grew up, what type of school he attended, or what were his interests and hobbies. The types of questions I would be asking him about would be about Mike Feeney the person and not Mike Feeney the worker at Biotech.

As I mentioned to you earlier, finding my leadership gene was an amazing discovery. It was something that I had inside of me that I never knew existed but had always remained dormant. My leadership gene remained dormant because it never really had a purpose to avail itself. I'm finding out that in life, having purpose has very little to do with self. Having purpose has much to do with others having purpose. I know that this doesn't make a lot of sense but is clear as a bell in my mind right now. I always thought that leadership was about "telling" and "doing." I was wrong. I was so wrong. Leadership is about setting example in finding a way to make possible visions and dreams that are only metaphors and excuses to others who dared not to dream because they doubt their own abilities to succeed. These individuals mask their insecurities by casting doubt on the ability of others to succeed who want to make their visions and dreams come true. The sad part of it all is often, they really don't know that they are doing this to others. Essentially, individuals who cast doubt on the ability of others are making their dreams come true and their visions come to fruition are really hurting inside. Perhaps someone along the way told them that they would never succeed because they couldn't follow orders correctly and they are not worth their own salt. It is clear in my mind that this is such a tragedy in knowing that so many people who had so much talent never had the ability to manifest that talent because of others who doubt their own abilities to manifest their talents.

It is clear as a bell in my mind now that connecting with people and understanding them and helping them make their dreams come true by listening to their visions of what is possible to them and not necessarily possible to me can be the difference between success and failure. I really don't know why I am thinking all of this right now. It is like something is coming out in the process of my existence that is raising me to a new level of consciousness that I could never have thought was possible. In a way, it is really scaring me. I never thought I had any of this inside of me. I never thought I could think this way. I am being raised to a whole new level of consciousness that is allowing me to see a bigger picture of myself than my job here at Biotech. I am not giving up in trying to find out from Russell the following. The first question I wanted to ask him was, why was Mike Feeney holding that manila envelope with the shoelace ties wrapped around it with his name on it that he took from him and me when I was unpacking the files to put in my office. Yes, all of the files that were compilations of Mike's, Lynn's, and my files. The second question I wanted to ask him would have to do with what was so important that Mike needed within the contents of the file. I am expecting that he is going to say that is absolutely none of my business. Yes, it is my business since it was in my office and put there for me to unpack. Clearly, this was something that he missed that ended up in a stray file box that I was never supposed to see. So why all the secrecy? Why was this file in Mike's hand when he died?

    In the past four years of Biotech, I would've never asked any of these questions. However, now I care. I care a lot more out of finding the truth of what happened with this organization. I care about all the employees that could potentially be affected by what I am observing right now before my eyes. What I observed has absolutely nothing to do with where I stand on the formal organizational grid. It has nothing to do with whom I report to or all who report to me. It has nothing to do with someone saying I am the boss and I am telling you to keep out of this. It has to do with individual lives and how it affects them, who depend on their salaries to make ends meet and live a quality of life that is conducive to the human connection in this company. Yes, my leadership gene is now manifesting itself and is now in full force.

I believe there is a reason for all this. I believe that I am in this place and time for a reason. I am realizing that leadership is much more than protocol, files, and downward communication. It is about purpose, vision, and mission, and it serves two masters. Let me explain what I mean about that. I believe that in life, there is a balance of two distinct elements of instinctive survival that everyone lives in their adult life. As a child, I was brought up to believe that everyone has values. I remember listening to Jonathan's story about how his sister brought him up when his mother passed away when he was at a very young age. His sister was everything to him, and she taught him good, solid values, which obviously rubbed off and caused him to be successful in life and in business. When he learned that his sister passed away, a piece of Jonathan also left him. This is why he was so devastated when he learned that she left him, physically that is. However, his sister's legacy continued to live on in him. Her legacy became part of his Contra. These values that he obtained from her and learned from her became one with him. Despite where Jonathan works for the rest of his life, the good, solid values he learned from his sister would always follow him and be a part of him. I remember in college, I learned about Maslow's hierarchy of needs. I also realized that getting a paycheck was on the bottom of the pyramid. For the longest time, getting a paycheck was at the top of my pyramid until I decided to go to California for an interview at another company. Apparently, getting a paycheck, according to Maslow, was a lower order need.

I believe now that by bringing out this leadership gene of connecting with people out of dormancy, I am beginning to fulfill a higher order need, which now is validating my ego. I am now realizing who I am, and I now have purpose. The second master that I mentioned was the organization. Despite everything that I believe about me, I have an obligation to help the organization that I work for to fulfill their mission. Did I really take the time to learn what Biotech was all about? Was I so concerned about protecting my own job and getting through the day-to-day functions than I was truly learning about why my company existed and the purpose it was fulfilling to make a difference in the lives of others? I think not. The most important part of everything here is finding a balance between my personal needs and the needs of the organization in which I work. The goal is to make a difference by finding that balance in both. Therefore, the hypotheses is that in plain English, if I am a happy camper and I am okay with myself and what I am doing in my organization, then the organization will succeed. I can make a difference and really have fun while I am doing my job. My job is no longer a burden and access only to making money. My job will be making a difference while I am making money in my life and in the life of others.

Finally, I am realizing this is not all about me. It is about everyone I interact with in my life inside and outside this organization. I also realized that I was exposed to all of these events for a reason. I am not suggesting that this is some supernatural occurrence. I really don't buy that type of stuff. However, I do realize that everyone existing on this planet is special whether I work for Biotech or not. I am realizing that everyone has some type of leadership gene in them that either manifests itself at one point in their life or remains dormant because it has no purpose to come out of that dormancy. When I think back of the movie *Contact* with Jodie Foster that I watched when I was sixteen years old, I remember when Jodie visited the planet Vega on some distant galaxy away from Earth. The figure she saw in the form of her dad whom she was very close to in life and lost at a very young age due to myocardial infarction (heart attack) said to her some very special words that always resonate in my mind, in one form or another. Those words were, "We are all very special. Each and every one of us is special. We have aspirations of either achieving." I'm not really sure of the words, but I have ideas in my head of what she said. Oh yes, she said something like this, "Your species has the ability to do amazing things and also destroy wonderful things." I believe it was something like that. I remember my dad played guitar and used to sing the song that came from the sixties. The song was written by a group called Youngblood. I believe the name of the song is "Get Together". I remember distinctly that one of the lines in the song went like this. Again, this is from memory. "You hold the keys to love and fear, and they are in your trembling hands. Though one key unlocks them both, they are at your command." I believe that in business, we make choices. We make choices to do things that we feel will have some type of benefit in the end. Whether that benefit is to destroy the dreams and aspirations of others, for personal greed and gain, or to see others succeed because we're making the difference of the keys that we hold in our hands. It is now four o'clock and still no Russell. I continued to work until five o'clock unpacking boxes. I looked up from my desk and just ready to go home, and who appears? Yes, the missing link is standing right in front of me before my eyes. Lynn Ann Marconi just flew in from LAX. She looked exhausted and smiled at me. I looked up at Lynn and said, "Why am I not surprised, you're here?"

Lynn looked up at me and said from the seat she was sitting in front of me, "I don't know, Josh, why don't you tell me."

Lynn's expression was much more relaxed, and she told me that Russell called the meeting with her and Jonathan for ten o'clock tomorrow morning in the conference room. She looked at me and said, "I thought you got an invitation, at least that's what Jonathan told me just before I left work." I looked at Lynn in amazement. I told her that I never got an invitation for that meeting. However, I did wonder why Jonathan and Russell were meeting with Mike Feeney earlier today. She said, "What are you talking about, Josh?" I looked at Lynn rather puzzled. Lynn said to me, "I thought the four of us would be getting together tomorrow morning to talk about Mike coming back and outline his duties with you." Lynn told me that she understood that Mike would be assisting me in getting the departments together, and she would provide the missing pieces while Mike was out of the office and away so we wouldn't break continuity. It was nothing more than that.

Abruptly, I said to Lynn, "Did you hear what happened to Mike today?"

Lynn looked at me in a very puzzled manner and said no, and then she stuttered and said, "Wha-what happened? Aren't we meeting tomorrow?"

I said to her, "You don't know, don't you?"

Lynn said, "Know, what?" I told Lynn that Mike passed away this morning. The reaction on her face was nothing like I've ever seen before. I thought she was going to pass out. I asked her if she wanted a glass of water, and she just shook her head no. I explained the whole story to her about my conversation with Russell and Jonathan earlier about the manila envelope with the shoelace-type ties wrapped around it with Mike's name on it. Lynn looked up at me and didn't miss a beat. However, the tears were filling up in her eyes, and she abruptly left my office and went to the ladies room.

Ten minutes later, Lynn came back from the ladies room and apologized for leaving so abruptly. I said to her, "Lynn, what do you know about all this?" She looked at me with tears in her eyes once again and said, "Maybe too much, Josh, maybe too much."

LEADERSHIP LESSONS

Josh appears to have found his leadership gene, although it took some extraordinary events to make him realize his potential. When we refer to the leadership gene, this is not something that some of us are born with and others lack it. Everyone has the gene, which is the potential to unite people to achieve a common goal. Finding the gene within ourselves is more difficult.

To find the gene within ourselves, we must learn to:

- envision the future and what is necessary to make it a reality,
- understand what the priorities are and maintain focus on them,
- be prepared for the unexpected and lead through adversity,
- control ourselves rather than trying to control others,
- understand how our behavior can affect others, both positively and negatively,
- accept emotions in ourselves and in others,
- focus on strengths rather than weaknesses in ourselves and in others,
- to be comfortable with candor, both as the provider and the recipient of feedback, and
- trust and be trustworthy at all times.

Chapter 12

THE HUMAN CONNECTION GENE MAKES ITS MARK

I said to her, "Lynn, what do you know about all this?"

She looked at me with tears in her eyes once again and said, "Maybe too much, Josh, maybe too much."

This is where we left off in the evening of the day Mike Feeney passed away. I looked at Lynn and said to her, "Are you hungry?"

She looked at me and said in a very disturbing voice, "How can you ask me a question like that at a time like this?"

I said to her, "I don't know. You traveled all day, and I just thought you might be hungry."

She looked up and said to me, "Josh, how can you possibly be so insensitive at a time like this? You just told me that Mike Feeney passed away and will not participate in a meeting I was going to sit in on with him and two other CEOs from two different pharmaceutical companies on opposite sides of the country."

I responded, "It was just a simple question, Lynn." I told her that it was just a gesture of hospitality, and I was shocked when I watched Mike Feeney die right before my eyes."

Lynn then opened her pocketbook to get some tissue to wipe her eyes from yet another emotional outburst, which was totally out of her character, at least how I knew her in the time that I worked with her. In the process of opening her pocketbook, a piece of paper fell on the floor, and I immediately went to grab it and picked it up, and she followed suit. However, I was a little bit quicker. I handed it back to her. She politely said thank you. Then, Lynn said to me, "Look, Josh, I really am sorry for overreacting." I nodded back to her that I understood it was okay, under the circumstances. For some reason, I just stopped talking and didn't say anything. I looked directly at Lynn and didn't say a word. I could feel myself making a connection with her that was much more collegial than adversarial. I felt that calmness come over me as it had several times before in times of crisis. It's something really that I can't explain. The feeling made me take control, not of others, but rather of myself. Most importantly, it helped me put everything into focus. The fear subsided from me, and the fog of uncertainty and insecurity was lifted. The feeling allowed me to see beyond what was going on at present and look into the future in which I can be empowered to make a positive difference.

I am now realizing the power of my leadership gene. It was probably one of the most powerful genes there in existence. This gene made a people connection. The gene looked beyond the body and penetrated the soul. In terms of Abraham Maslow, it reached the higher order needs. It looked beyond what existed and offered hope to what is possible. It looked for true colors in people and offered solutions rather than criticisms. The gene made one feel good about himself or herself and did the same in others. I now know what I want from Lynn. I wanted the truth. I wanted to know what she knew about Mike Feeney, Josh, and, perhaps, even Jonathan. My silence continued, and my stare became more intense as my calmness persisted.

 Lynn looked up at me and finally said, "You know, Josh, you're right. I am getting a little hungry, and I'm very tired. Let's go out and get something to eat." I looked at Lynn, and I knew I'd finally get through to her. She was making the connection with me. Just like the song says that was discussed earlier, "You hold the keys to love and fear. They're in your trembling hands. Though one key unlocks them both, they are at your command."

 On the way to Café Roberto in the North End of Boston, I told Lynn all about that little place Jonathan and I visited at the airport in LAX. I explained to her how many different types of pasta there was to choose from in that exclusive Italian restaurant. We were like a couple of teenagers laughing, joking, and chuckling all the way to Roberto's, seemingly without a care in the world. I really began to learn about Lynn from a human perspective. She was a kind and gentle person who had worked her way through college and the only child of very poor parents. She worked two jobs while putting herself through school and never got into a serious relationship because she didn't have the time. She told me that sometimes she regretted not settling down and starting a family, but she truly loved her work. She considered the employees who work with her at Medical Solutions like family. She told me while she was here at Biotech, although a very short time, she considered everyone to be family.

We finally got a seat at Roberto's after about a twenty-minute wait, which wasn't so bad for midevening in a Boston restaurant. I always communicated with Lynn as my boss and not my colleague. Our relationship was always much more subservient than it was collegial. I guess this was part of a culture that we accept but never really analyze. On the formal organizational grid, we have a reporting protocol. We accept that protocol as subservient and obedient to our superiors. We never really look at our supervisors as human beings first, then our bosses second. It is usually the other way around. Now that I think of it, often organizations do not communicate properly because they are more interested in satisfying the position that a person holds rather than the task of problem that needed to be addressed in environments that were governed through shared leadership.

Shared leadership should not be confused with formal leadership. These are two very different things. Shared leadership is about collegial bonding that looks beyond satisfying an end to a means. In other words, the focus is on the process rather than the fear of not meeting the end result because the boss will be unhappy with us. I know this may sound kind of strange to you right now. However, I am going to a different place in my relationship, first with myself and second with the individuals I associate with at my company. I realized that I can still address Lynn as my supervisor if she were still my boss but also retain the autonomy of working with her as a colleague to solve a problem within the context of the organizational structure. In the past, I had often found myself only finishing a job on time are doing things efficiently to please Mike, Lynn, or whomever I reported to at the time.

Shared leadership is a lot different. It is built on mutual respect for having the ability to seek answers and provide solutions to problems. It ignores the "boss/subordinate" relationship and only seeks resolution by neither party, boss or subordinate, dominating a process just because they have higher rank on the organizational grid. I believe that this is where leadership should be going. It should be focusing on successorship of performing tasks to satisfy organizational and personal needs and not individual egos. It is about mutual respect for all parties, despite their role in the organization to treat others as intellectual equals and an intrinsic component and supporter of the organizational mission and goals.

Lynn is finally getting settled at her seat as the maître d' helps position Lynn adjacent to a lovely table for two covered with a linen tablecloth under a centerpiece of long candlesticks giving ambient light inserted into a gold candelabra. Lynn looked up at me and said, "It doesn't get better than this, Josh! Thank you so much for helping me put it all in perspective." I looked at Lynn and again felt that calmness coming over me, and I didn't say anything after her comment. Suddenly, the entire contour of her face changed as if she were schizophrenic, going from one personality to another. Her face got very somber and serious, and her eyes filled once again.

Instinctively, I grabbed Lynn's hand. Her hand was cold and clammy, and her lips were trembling. Again, the calmness continued to permeate through my body. I was focused and could not be distracted by anything around me at this time. The tears were now beginning to flow down Lynn's cheeks, and she went to her pocketbook to grab some tissue paper. I immediately grabbed that free hand and prevented her from taking her focus off my face. This time, I'm the one who said, "What?" Her lips were trembling even more, and she couldn't speak. The tears continued to flow down her cheeks. I signaled to the maître d' to get some water over to our table. He immediately gestured to one of the waiters who came over with a pitcher full of ice water and poured some in a glass and gave it to Lynn.

I thanked him, and he said, "I'll be back in a minute to take your order. My name is Carlos." I told him to give us a few minutes, and I would signal for him when we were ready. He smiled and walked away.

Lynn guzzled down the water as if she were a camel in the middle of the desert, discovering an oasis after walking for three days in scorching sun. I poured her another glass of iced water from the pitcher and gently grabbed her other hand and offered her my clean handkerchief to wipe her eyes from the tears that were falling freely. This time, I was very gentle with her, and I understood that I would be the one she would tell about the scandal that she kept in for so long and swore she would never tell anyone. I instinctively understood that she trusted me with her entire life at this time. I couldn't explain why, but we made a connection that was beyond work, beyond friendship, and that answered to a higher level. You see, we were both seeking to release the true inner selves that we both kept dormant for so long. This wasn't about us. This wasn't about a relationship that existed between a man and a woman. This was about doing the right thing so that many would benefit and learn from in the process. It was about putting fear aside and not worrying about personal consequences to the actions we might have to take once the truth was discovered.

Some believe that there is karma or a guiding principle that helps us make decisions in life and puts us at the right place at the right time because we are the right people to solve problems we would never think possible. This may be true. However, there is nothing that we can do to make change unless we make a conscious effort to take the risk that is necessary because we believe it is the right thing to do. We are all subservient to our own actions and really in the end only answer to ourselves. Right or wrong, good or bad, we are accountable to ourselves to do the right thing. Whatever we perceive that to be, right now I am focused on doing the right thing.

Lynn looked at me and said, "I'm a mess, Josh, maybe you should just take me back to my hotel, and I'll see you tomorrow." Again, the calmness stayed with me, and I didn't say anything. I continued to hold both her hands, and I could feel our hands pulsating at the same time. I felt that we were in sync and the calmness of my demeanor and the heat from my hands were beginning to calm her down, and the trembling eventually subsided.

I continued to look at her in a deep stare, and I gently said, "What has been eating you for so long, Lynn?" I paused for a second and waited for a response. Just at that time, the waiter came to our table to take our order.

Lynn looked up at me and said, "I'm really not that hungry, Josh."

I smiled and looked at her and I said, "Well, I'm starving, and I'm going to eat. You can just sit there and watch me if you want."

The waiter looked at me, smiled, and said, "I can still give you another minute and come back if you want, sir."

I looked at him, and I looked at Lynn and said, "No, that won't be necessary. We'll give you our order now." I said this with certainty abruptness and did not even look Lynn in the eye when I made the statement. I gave the maître d' my order and looked at Lynn and said, "He's ready to take your order now." Lynn smiled at me and gave the waiter her order. We sat in silence for the next ten minutes while we were waiting for our order to be prepared. Lynn was checking her e-mails, and I was doing the same thing. Coincidentally, we both looked up at each other at the same time, and our eyes locked once again.

Lynn looked at me with a grimace on her forehead and said, "Okay, the truth."

"I want you to know I have been working for Jonathan for about four years in LA at Medical Solutions as the chief financial officer and not what I told you when I met you and your team for the first time. I couldn't tell you the truth for obvious reasons. I am not a thirty-two-year-old mother of two children. I had not been with a company for eleven years in Wisconsin before I came to work at Biotech. I was really good at my job, and I was up for promotion. There was an open slot for director of operations at Medical Solutions. I thought I would be a shoe-in for the job."

I continued to listen attentively to Lynn as she continued her story shortly after the delicious food arrived. During dinner, she continued her story without missing a beat. She was reliving the whole experience of policy transitioned over to Biotech. Lynn explained to me that going back six months. She recalled listening again on a conversation between Jonathan and Russell. Jonathan was here at LAX at Medical Solutions and Russell in Boston at Biotech. She told me how interesting the conversation was, and she overheard them having a very loud and heated debate on the telephone. She told me that she didn't pay much attention to the debate as she was focused on her work and tried not to stick her nose into anything that didn't concern her. She told me that the next thing she knew, Jonathan came out of his office and came into hers and said with a nervous chuckle, "We weren't too loud in there, were we, Lynn?" Lynn told me that she chuckled back at Jonathan and stated she wasn't even paying the slightest bit of attention to their conversation. She told me that Jonathan then became serious and said to her, "Russell is flying in to LA tomorrow morning. Do you mind picking him up at the airport?" I looked at Lynn rather inquisitively and told her to continue as I wiped the last morsel of dinner from my lips.

Lynn looked at me and chuckled and said, "Jonathan said, 'When Russell arrives and we go into our meeting, I would like you to join us and bring your ledger for all of our key accounts over the past six months. Additionally, I would like you to also bring all the records of all our generic and brand-name drugs into the room.'" At this point, Lynn's lips started trembling. Once again, I offered her water, and she nodded her head and told me she was okay. We were now waiting for our dessert and finished. Lynn told me she had enough money in her expense account to take care of the bill. I thanked her, and we left the restaurant. As we left walking out the door, Lynn looked at me and said, "Josh, are you tired?" I must admit I became a little nervous at this point, not knowing what she was going with this conversation.

Again, I put my fears aside; calmness took over my body, and I looked at Lynn and said, "Not necessarily. What do you have in mind?"

Lynn said to me, "It's a beautiful evening. Let's walk along the beach. I really want to finish my story while I have the courage to do so. You have the right to know what really happened at Biotech and what was in that folder that Mike Feeney held on the day he died."

LEADERSHIP LESSONS

Josh has grasped the concept of shared leadership. While we can't escape formal lines of authority within a business organization (yet), we see the effectiveness of the concept in other arenas. For example, a professional sports team has an owner and a formal management structure. On the field, however, direction comes from those who understand the current situation, the options available, and the objective. Individuals at all positions bring their knowledge, experience, and talents together to achieve the objective.

In sports and in business, everyone on a team has a different view of a situation. By communicating with each other, they can achieve great things together.

Chapter 13

MY LEADERSHIP GENE AND I ARE ONE

My response to Lynn was, "Let's move on then!" I wanted now to put the pieces of the puzzle together and know how I fit into this whole equation. I was really curious but at the same time wanted to find out what Lynn knew and why Mike Feeney died. I needed to know a little bit more about my mentor, Jonathan, and the CEO of the company I worked for, Russell.

It was now about 10:30 in the evening, and it was beautiful. The temperature was about seventy degrees, the humidity was low, and the air was crisp. I felt very comfortable being with Lynn. She was a real and genuine individual who cared about people beyond herself. Lynn was struggling with life. Just as I was and just as Jonathan seems to be, perhaps even Mike Feeney. When we arrived at the beach, we both took our shoes and socks off and decided to walk barefooted along the cool, crisp sand and decided to get close to the ocean and watch the waves roll away and out. The moon was just beautiful. It was a three quarter moon. where you'd swear you'll be able to see right into the craters. The light reflected off the moon from the sun glistening on the ocean's highest points as the waves came trickling in and out.

For a fleeting moment, we were in harmony with nature, and everything became so crystal clear in my head. I stood beside the ocean, and I realized how small I was, and I never wanted to forget that I was only a very small piece in a very big puzzle. Yet I also realized that what I was seeking to learn would help put everything back in order that had been misaligned for so long at Biotech. I watched the alignment of the sun's rays on the moon's reflection that lit up the ocean, and that beacon of light had guided many ships to land hundreds of years ago. You see, the moon's light highlighted the algae in the ocean, signaling that land was near to many sailors who we'd been at sea for months.

As Lynn and I began walking, she continued her story. Lynn explained to me that when she joined Russell and Jonathan with her ledger at the closed-door meeting the next day after Russell arrived, they presented a copy to her of the drug they have been working on with research and developments at Biotech that reflected a major breakthrough for treating children with attention deficit disorder, better known as ADD. The drug that was presently used was a class A drug and extremely expensive. The breakthrough would cost only a third of the cost of the present drug and was proven to work. Lynn, as she continued her story, acknowledged the fact that Jonathan and Russell went to school together and had been friends for years. They went their separate ways, and both ended up as CEOs in their respective companies. Both had very promising futures, and this new discovery would be a great way of putting them on the map, in addition to making them both very wealthy.

Jonathan and Russell new that it would take at least a year before the new drug would be approved by the Federal Drug Administration (FDA), and they could not live with the twelve months they would have to wait to get this new drug on the market. Additionally, the competition would have an entire year to come up with the same drug, and this would further increase the risk that the new drug would not be attractive to the shareholders at Biotech. Lynn further explained to me that she questioned why Medical Solutions would be concerned if Biotech made the discovery. It was explained to Lynn that many of the shareholders that sat on both Medical Solutions's and Biotech's board of directors had similar vested interests in the new drug. She explained Russell and Jonathan did not go into any more detail with her, and Russell was giving Jonathan dirty looks for even saying that much to Lynn.

At this point, my curiosity was peaked, and I was beginning to catch on rather quickly. I was listening to a scandal being uncovered right before my very years and eyes. However, I retained my calmness and asked Lynn to continue her story. We had already walked about a mile down the beach, and it was after 11:30 p.m. We kept walking and talking. Mostly, it was Lynn talking. I was doing the listening.

She stated she was directed to make a call to Mike Feeney, director of operations at Biotech, and tell him to contact his connection at the FDA. Lynn told me that this was about a month before she came to Biotech as interim director of operations. Lynn went on to explain (as she said to make a long story short), Michael was told to ask his connection active at the FDA to push through the new drug as soon as possible without going through all the rigorous testing that is required for final approval given by the FDA, which usually takes about a year. I was told that Mike refused to make the call and would not compromise his integrity. I told Lynn that it was my understanding that Mike's health was failing, and that's why he was told to leave and taken out of his position. She told me that there was some truth to this, but it wasn't severe enough to ground him from doing his job.

I told Lynn at this point that I was really getting confused and none of this made sense. I asked Lynn how I fit into this picture going for my interview at Medical Solutions, which was of my own free will because I was unhappy the way Mike was treating me at Biotech. Lynn chuckled and said to me that I played right into their plan perfectly. She immediately came back with a correction to her last statement and said, "Jonathan and Russell's plan. It was not mine. I was just a pawn on the chessboard."

Lynn went on to explain that when Mike refused to compromise his integrity by asking his contact at the FDA to move up the release date of the new drug, he was given the option of being terminated or resign with a generous severance package. "The company would just state he resigned due to poor health. Mike was given twenty-four hours to make up his mind. He was told in either case, he would be replaced by me. You see, they wanted me to replace Mike because I already knew too much. Lynn stated she was told to keep an eye on me at Biotech, just in case Mike tried to tell me anything about what was going on between Russell and Jonathan. And it was also important that I keep an eye on the ledger and protect our interests and the new drug."

I then said to Lynn, "I still don't get how I fit into the picture. Since I went on my own free will to Medical Solutions for an interview after the way Mike had been treating me before you came and how different you were to have as a boss. I felt no challenge in Biotech any longer, and I needed a change. No one prompted me to do this." Lynn told me that this was all true. But the circumstances led me directly from Biotech to Medical Solutions. Lynn explained to me that Mike's obnoxious behavior toward me was due to the fact that he was under such pressure to do things that were totally unethical in an environment that he had been working in for most of his professional career. Then, she explained that she came along and wasn't different toward anything that I was doing and had a different demeanor than with anyone I have ever worked with at Biotech. She explained to me that she heard I was interviewing for jobs when she got a call from Jonathan in LA, stating that his secretary had received my resumé. Of course, she explained that she had given a list of all employees that Mike Feeney had as direct reports to him to Jonathan and assurance that none of the news leaked out about the scandal. She explained that there was no chance; I would be denied an interview from Jonathan since I worked for Mike Feeney. She told me that Jonathan, if he had interviewed me, would've pumped me for what I know about Mike Feeney and anything that had to do with research and development at Biotech. Lynn told me that as soon as she got the heads-up that I would be traveling to LA for an interview with Jonathan, she was to meet him at the airport and distract me, saying she was going to meet someone else there. In reality, she told me she was there at the airport to meet Russell, who never showed up as his plane was delayed. She needed to get back to Biotech to meet Russell and Jonathan for a meeting with Mike Feeney. Obviously, that never happened.

I then asked Lynn, "Then was it really true that Jonathan's sister had passed away?" Lynn looked up at me and stood facing me and pulled back from me at arm's length. She reached out her hands and grabbed my hands facing me. Her eyes filled with tears, once again. This time, she was not trembling. Lynn looked at me in total silence as her eyes met mine. Instinctively, we both turned our heads, and we looked at the bright light of the moon reflecting on the snowcaps of the waves as they were coming into the shore. When the waves rolled in, the calm ocean water gently settled on our feet before receding back into the ocean. Lynn said softly to me, "Jonathan's sister did pass away, and that was the part of our plan that was not planned. His sister's passing changed his entire life and stopped his tracks." She said that he really needed something like this to happen to make him realize where he came from, what his values were, and how greed can change an individual from a kind soul and a hardworking person to a monster almost overnight.

I immediately put it altogether, and now it all made sense. The real Jonathan came through when we met at that Italian restaurant in LA. In retrospect, the real story came through on the beach with Lynn at an Italian restaurant in Boston.

I asked Lynn the two final questions. "What did Mike Feeney have in his hand that I wasn't supposed to see when I unpacked everyone's files?"

Lynn looked at me and said, "Oh, that. It was a letter that Jonathan had written to Mike Feeney's FDA contact explaining that he was withdrawing his request to move up the date for releasing the new drug without going through all the proper tests and would be happy to abide to any consequences resulting from his actions. He also explained that Mike Feeney had absolutely nothing to do with any of this." I asked Lynn if there was more because she didn't seem like she was finished. Lynn looked at me very gently with her hands still outstretched meeting mine and abruptly pulled us closer and dropped her hands by her side. Lynn said, "Yes, Josh, there is more. In the letter, Jonathan stated that he learned a valuable lesson about himself and who he was that reminded him of a close relationship he had with an individual he once loved very much who brought him up and helped make him successful. This was his sister, who had just died. He said, he met a young man who was supposed to interview with him for a job and taught him that leadership is about people and not about money. Finally, in his letter, he stated that he would be resigning from his position as CEO of Medical Solutions.

I stood there speechless with my mouth open, not knowing how to respond to Lynn. When I finally gain my composure, I said to Lynn, "If Jonathan resigned from

Medical Solutions, then why we are here in Boston to meet with Russell and Jonathan today?" I then went on to ask her, "I wonder who will be the next CEO of Medical Solutions if Jonathan resigned."

Lynn looked at me and didn't say anything for about five seconds and then put her arms around my neck and whispered in my ear, "You're looking at her." I stood there speechless with my mouth opened as she pulled away from me and grinned from ear to ear. I said to Lynn, "Why were you getting so emotional then when we were going out to dinner?" She put her head down and looked at the sand.

When she raised her head once again, she said to me, "You still don't get it, do you? The untimely death of Mike Feeney was devastating to me. However, you connected with me and made me realize that it was okay. I could take on this new challenge, and I could go on."

I looked at her, and this time my eyes filled. I said to her, "Thank you so much for believing in me. I didn't realize that I influenced your life and Jonathan's life in such a manner until now."

Finally, Lynn said to me, "I believe in you so much, Josh, that I want you to come with me to Medical Solutions to be my new director of operations if you'll allow me to work with you as a trusted colleague, friend, and welcome in a new culture for our industry."

I said, "What happens to Russell at this point?"

Lynn looked at me and smiled and said, "Don't you remember about that book I gave you entitled *Leadership Is a Choice*?" I told her I do remember that book.

Lynn chuckled and said, "Read it, and that will answer your question."

REFERENCES

Contact is a 1997 science fiction drama film adapted from the Carl Sagan novel of the same name and directed by Robert Zemeckis. Both Sagan and wife Ann Druy...

"Get Together" is a '60s song written by the folk group Young Bloods, which was released in 1966 and recorded from RCA Victor in 1969. The song was also recorded by the Kingston Trio.

www.ingramcontent.com/pod-product-compliance
Lightning Source LLC
Chambersburg PA
CBHW071734080526
44588CB00013B/2033